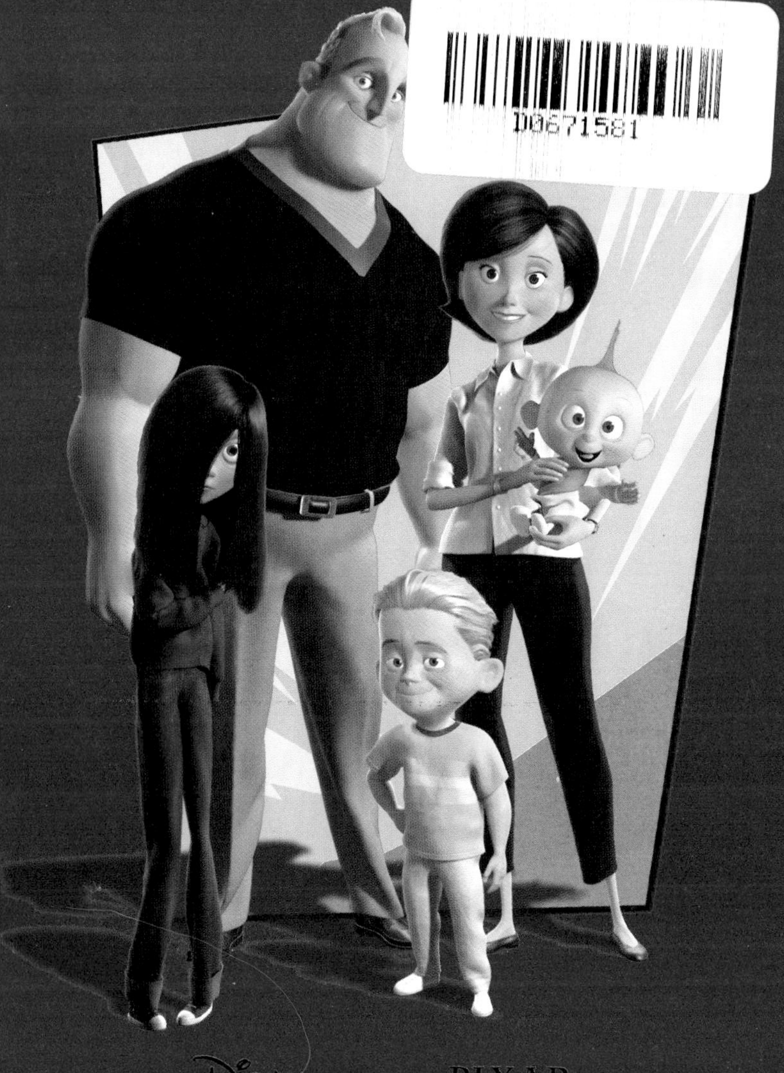

Disney presents a PIXAR film

THE INCREDIBLES

TOKYOPOP®
HAMBURG • LONDON • LOS ANGELES • TOKYO

Editor - Erin Stein
Contributing Editor - Amy Court-Kaemon
Graphic Designers and Letterers - Anna Kernbaum, Tomás Montalvo-Lagos,
and Jennifer Nunn-Iwai
Cover Designer - Anna Kernbaum
Graphic Artists - Louis Csontos and Monalisa de Asis

Production Managers - Jennifer Miller and Mutsumi Miyazaki
Senior Designer - Anna Kernbaum
Art Director - Matt Alford
Senior Editor - Elizabeth Hurchalla
Managing Editor - Jill Freshney
VP of Production - Ron Klamert
Editor in Chief - Mike Kiley
President & C.O.O. - John Parker
Publisher & C.E.O. - Stuart Levy

E-mail: info@tokyopop.com
Come visit us online at www.TOKYOPOP.com

A 🔲TOKYOPOP® Cine-Manga® Book
TOKYOPOP Inc.
5900 Wilshire Blvd., Suite 2000
Los Angeles, CA 90036

The Incredibles

DISNEP PRESENTS A PIXAR FILM

THE INCREDIBLES

ISBN: 1-59532-720-7

First TOKYOPOP® printing: March 2005

10 9 8 7 6 5 4 3 2

Printed in the USA

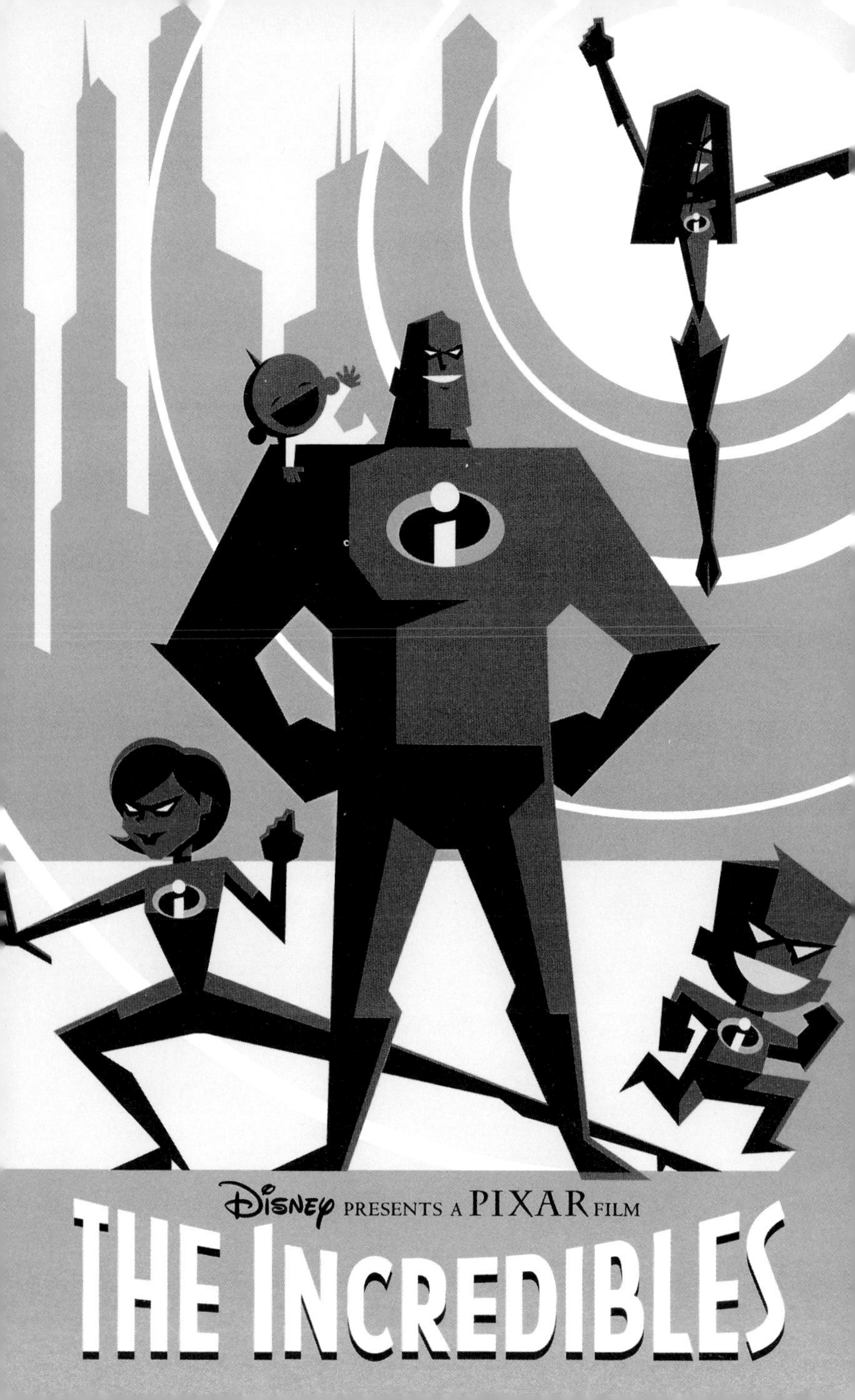
Disney PRESENTS A PIXAR FILM
THE INCREDIBLES

Who are the SUPERS?

Violet Parr has the power of invisibility and can throw force fields, though she mostly just tries to blend in.

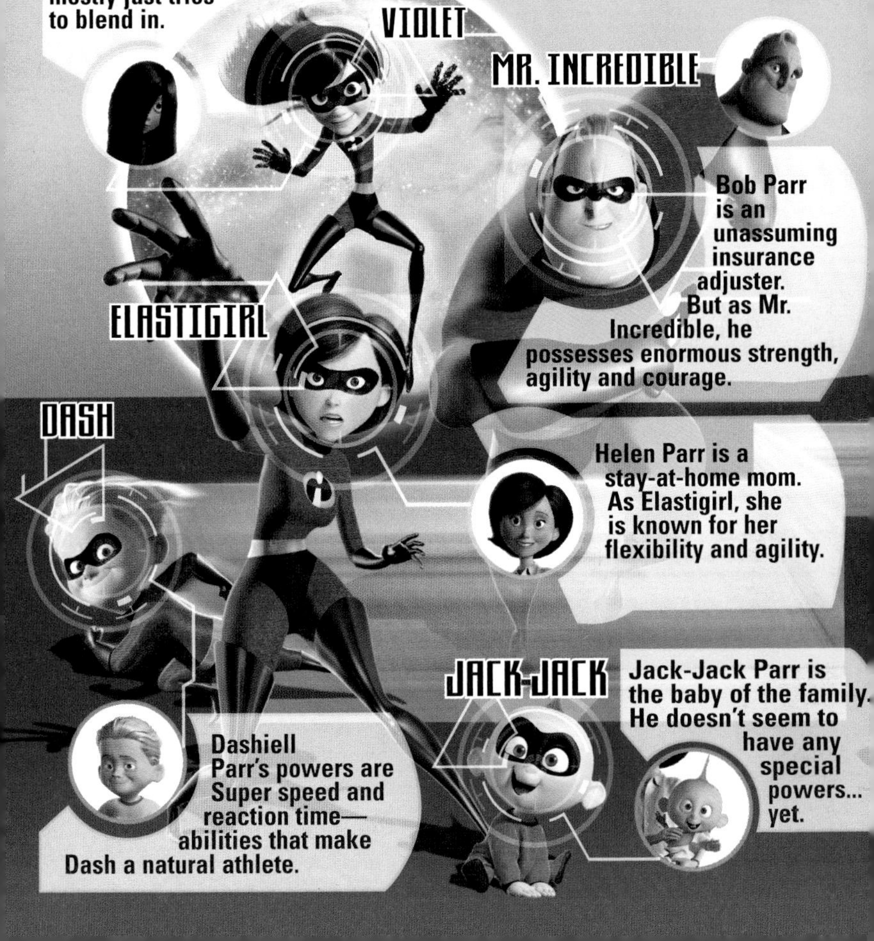
VIOLET
MR. INCREDIBLE
ELASTIGIRL
DASH
JACK-JACK

Bob Parr is an unassuming insurance adjuster. But as Mr. Incredible, he possesses enormous strength, agility and courage.

Helen Parr is a stay-at-home mom. As Elastigirl, she is known for her flexibility and agility.

Dashiell Parr's powers are Super speed and reaction time—abilities that make Dash a natural athlete.

Jack-Jack Parr is the baby of the family. He doesn't seem to have any special powers... yet.

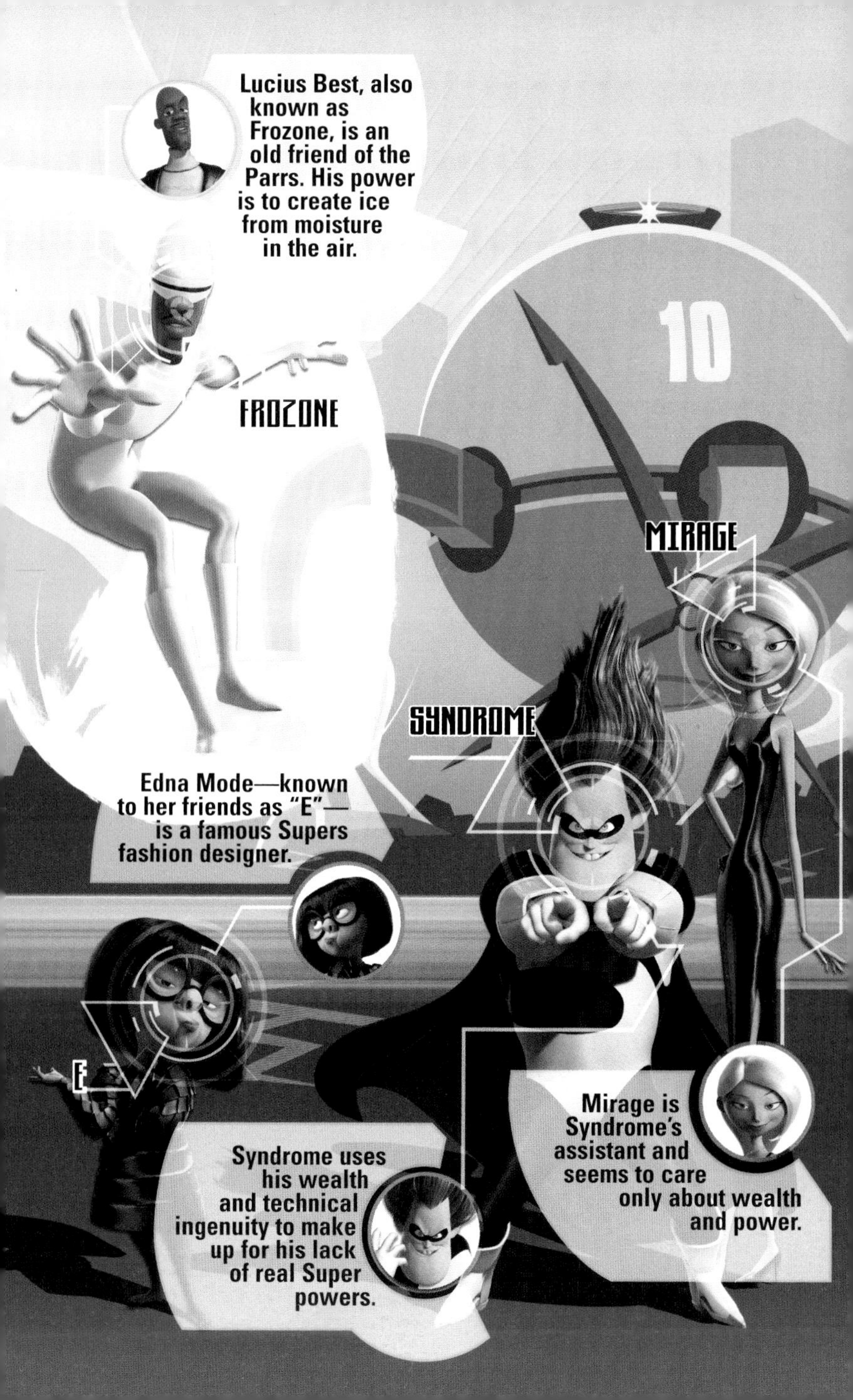

Lucius Best, also known as Frozone, is an old friend of the Parrs. His power is to create ice from moisture in the air.

FROZONE

MIRAGE

SYNDROME

Edna Mode—known to her friends as "E"— is a famous Supers fashion designer.

E

Syndrome uses his wealth and technical ingenuity to make up for his lack of real Super powers.

Mirage is Syndrome's assistant and seems to care only about wealth and power.

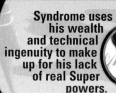

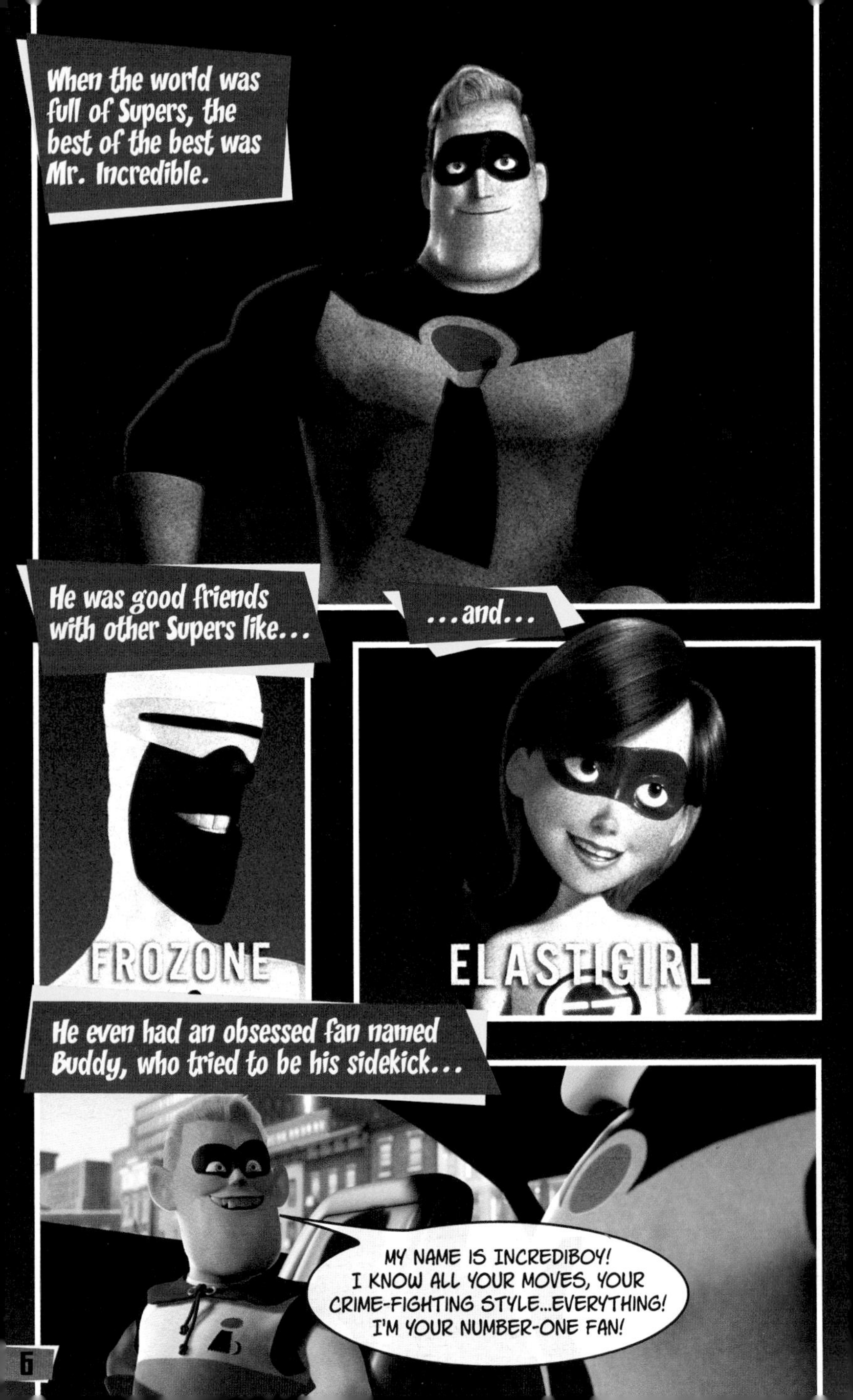

When the world was full of Supers, the best of the best was Mr. Incredible.
He was good friends with other Supers like...
...and...
FROZONE
ELASTIGIRL
He even had an obsessed fan named Buddy, who tried to be his sidekick...
MY NAME IS INCREDIBOY! I KNOW ALL YOUR MOVES, YOUR CRIME-FIGHTING STYLE...EVERYTHING! I'M YOUR NUMBER-ONE FAN!

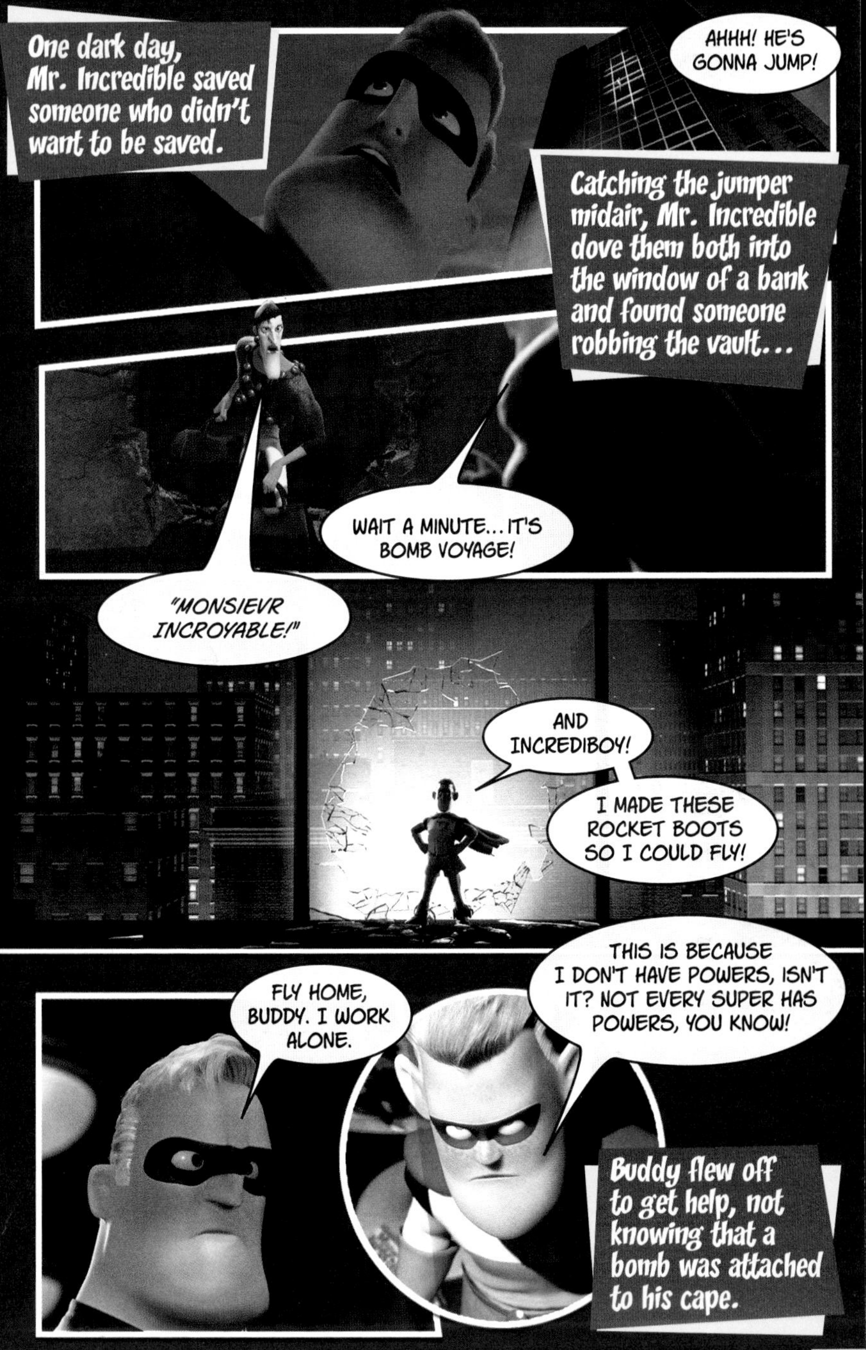
One dark day, Mr. Incredible saved someone who didn't want to be saved.
AHHH! HE'S GONNA JUMP!
Catching the jumper midair, Mr. Incredible dove them both into the window of a bank and found someone robbing the vault...
WAIT A MINUTE... IT'S BOMB VOYAGE!
"MONSIEVR INCROYABLE!"
AND INCREDIBOY!
I MADE THESE ROCKET BOOTS SO I COULD FLY!
FLY HOME, BUDDY. I WORK ALONE.
THIS IS BECAUSE I DON'T HAVE POWERS, ISN'T IT? NOT EVERY SUPER HAS POWERS, YOU KNOW!
Buddy flew off to get help, not knowing that a bomb was attached to his cape.

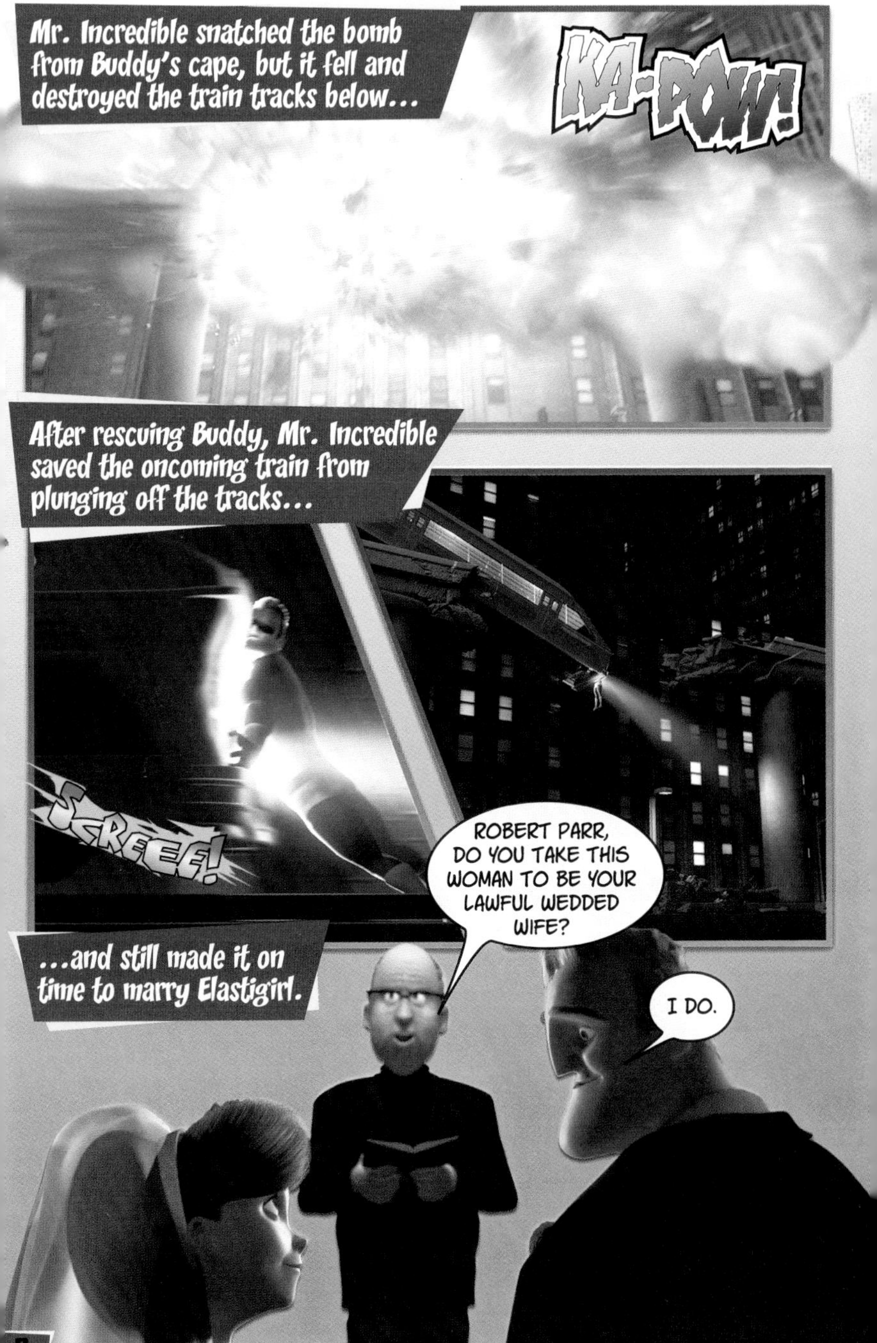
Mr. Incredible snatched the bomb from Buddy's cape, but it fell and destroyed the train tracks below...
KA-POW!
After rescuing Buddy, Mr. Incredible saved the oncoming train from plunging off the tracks...
SCREEE!
ROBERT PARR, DO YOU TAKE THIS WOMAN TO BE YOUR LAWFUL WEDDED WIFE?
...and still made it on time to marry Elastigirl.
I DO.

Then something terrible happened...

Metroville Tribu

Mr. Incredible Gets Sued

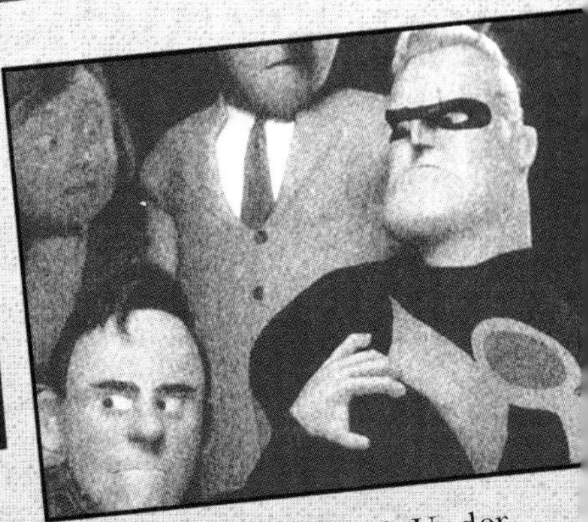

In a stunning turn of events, a Super is being sued for saving someone who—apparently—didn't want to be saved. Under tremendous public pressure, the government initiated the Super Relocation Program. The Supers would be granted amnesty from responsibility for past actions in exchange for the promise to never again resume hero work.

Continued on page 14.

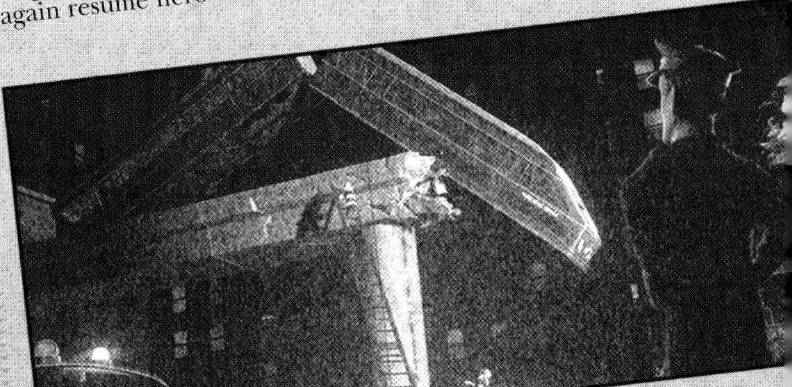

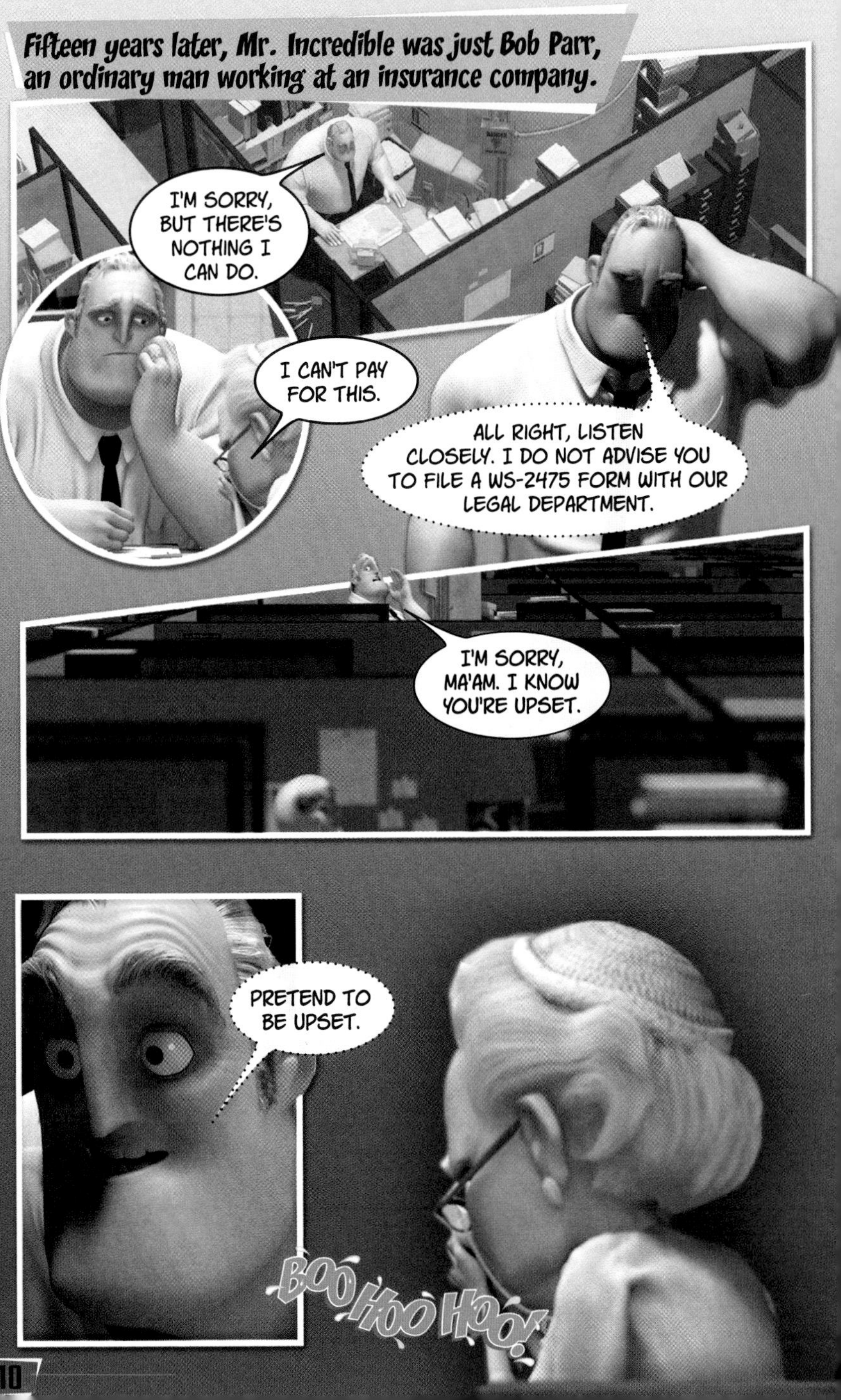
Fifteen years later, Mr. Incredible was just Bob Parr, an ordinary man working at an insurance company.
I'M SORRY, BUT THERE'S NOTHING I CAN DO.
I CAN'T PAY FOR THIS.
ALL RIGHT, LISTEN CLOSELY. I DO NOT ADVISE YOU TO FILE A WS-2475 FORM WITH OUR LEGAL DEPARTMENT.
I'M SORRY, MA'AM. I KNOW YOU'RE UPSET.
PRETEND TO BE UPSET.
BOO HOO HOO!

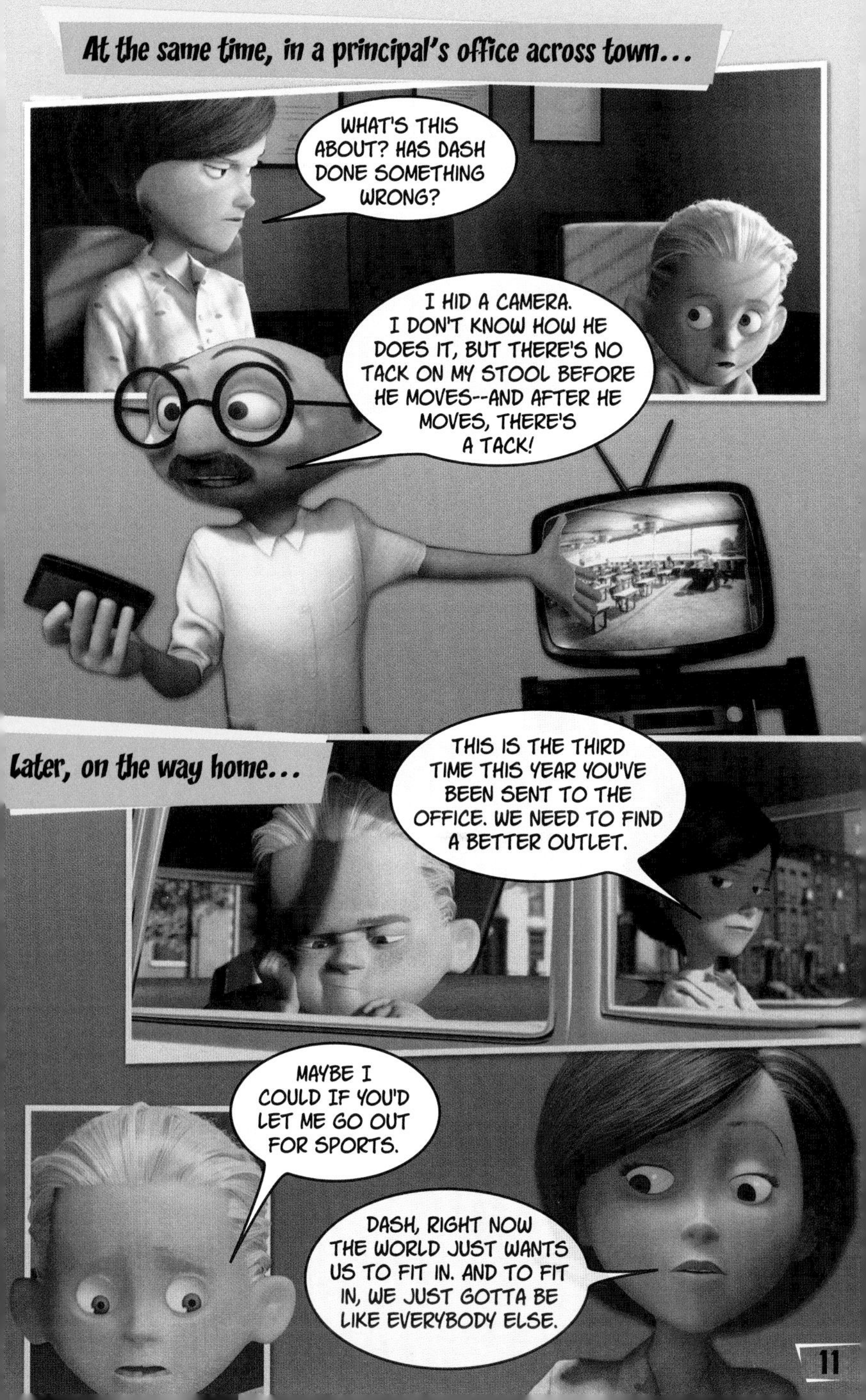

At the same time, in a principal's office across town...
WHAT'S THIS ABOUT? HAS DASH DONE SOMETHING WRONG?
I HID A CAMERA. I DON'T KNOW HOW HE DOES IT, BUT THERE'S NO TACK ON MY STOOL BEFORE HE MOVES--AND AFTER HE MOVES, THERE'S A TACK!
Later, on the way home...
THIS IS THE THIRD TIME THIS YEAR YOU'VE BEEN SENT TO THE OFFICE. WE NEED TO FIND A BETTER OUTLET.
MAYBE I COULD IF YOU'D LET ME GO OUT FOR SPORTS.
DASH, RIGHT NOW THE WORLD JUST WANTS US TO FIT IN. AND TO FIT IN, WE JUST GOTTA BE LIKE EVERYBODY ELSE.

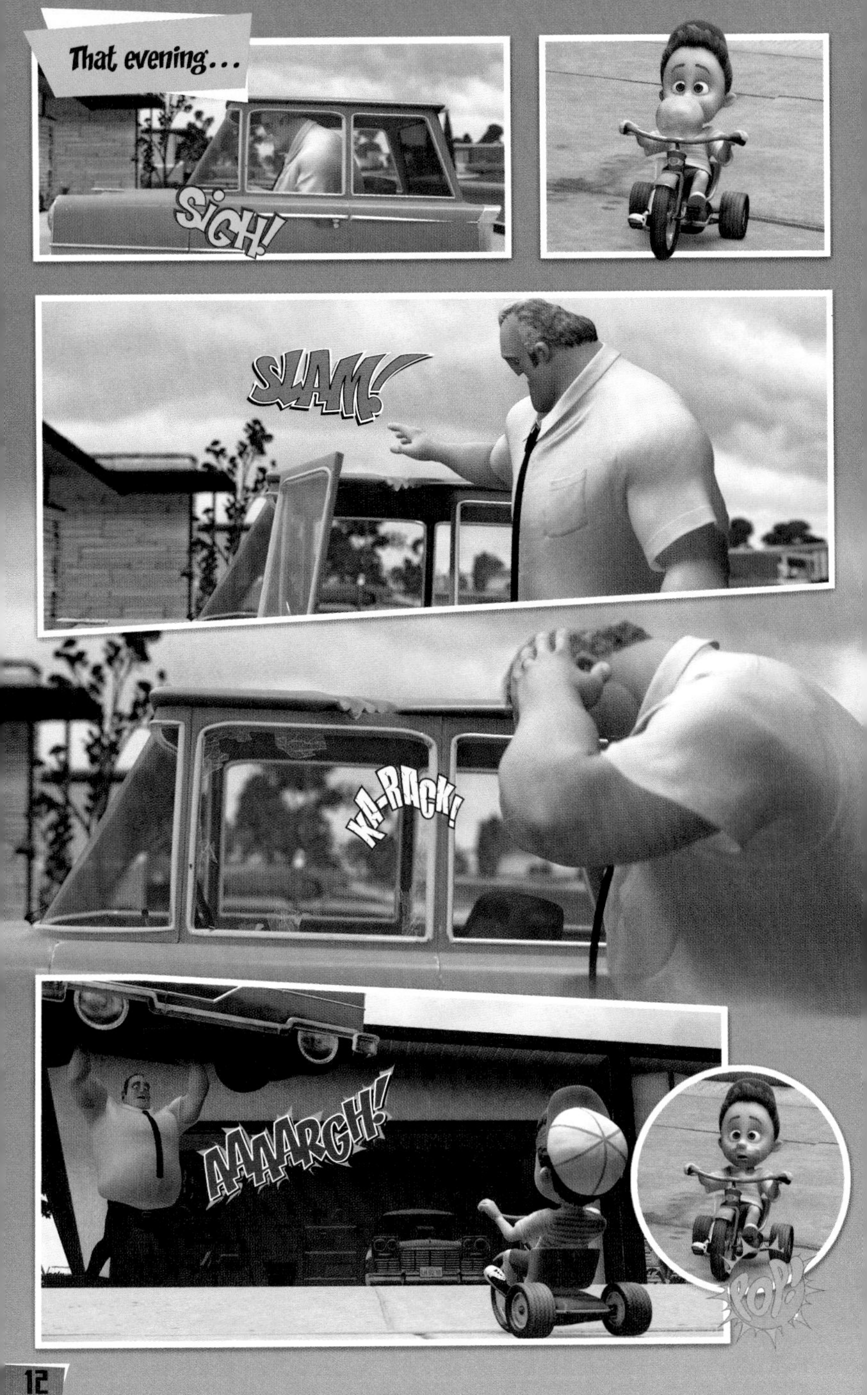
That evening...
SIGH!
SLAM!
KA-RACK!
AAAARGH!
POP!

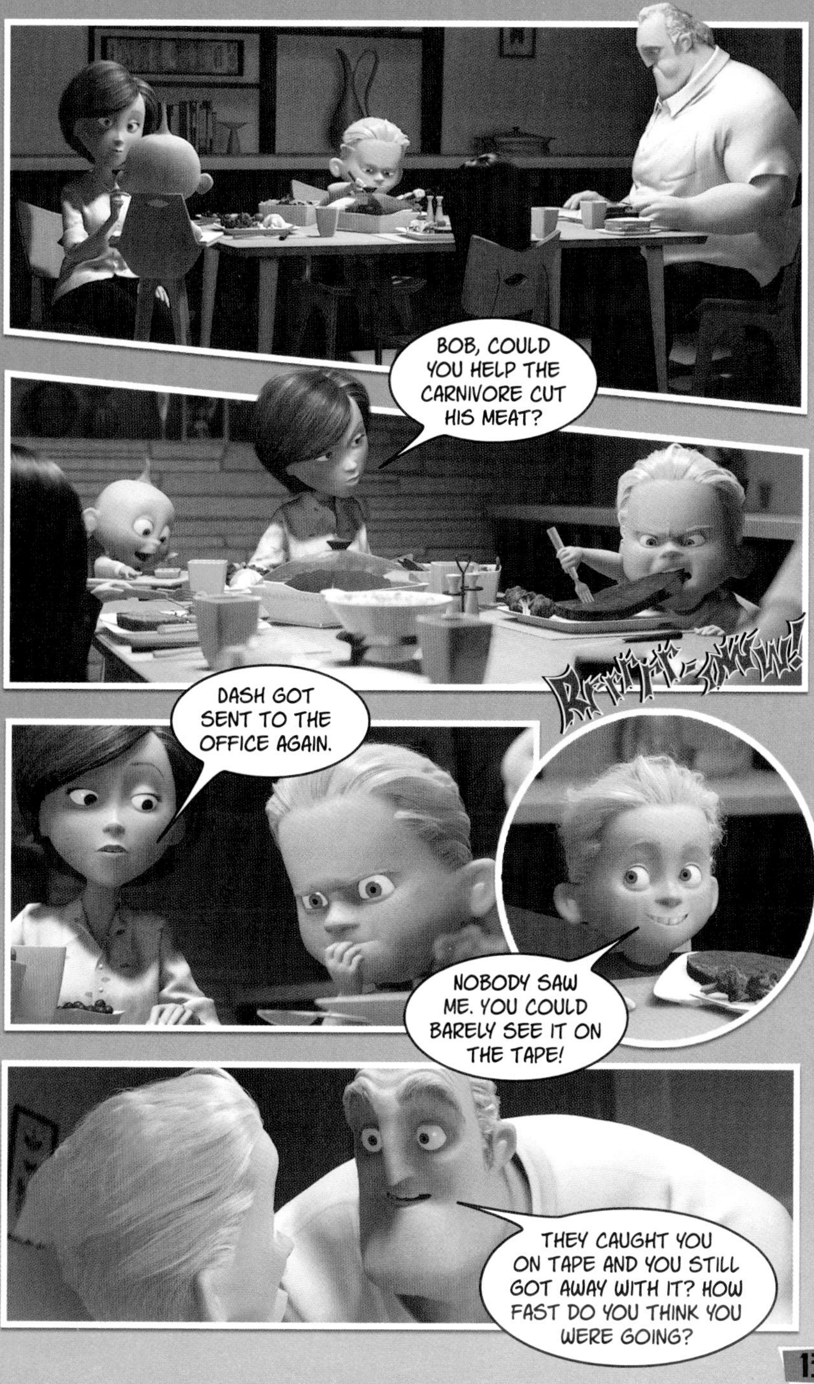
BOB, COULD YOU HELP THE CARNIVORE CUT HIS MEAT?
DASH GOT SENT TO THE OFFICE AGAIN.
NOBODY SAW ME. YOU COULD BARELY SEE IT ON THE TAPE!
THEY CAUGHT YOU ON TAPE AND YOU STILL GOT AWAY WITH IT? HOW FAST DO YOU THINK YOU WERE GOING?

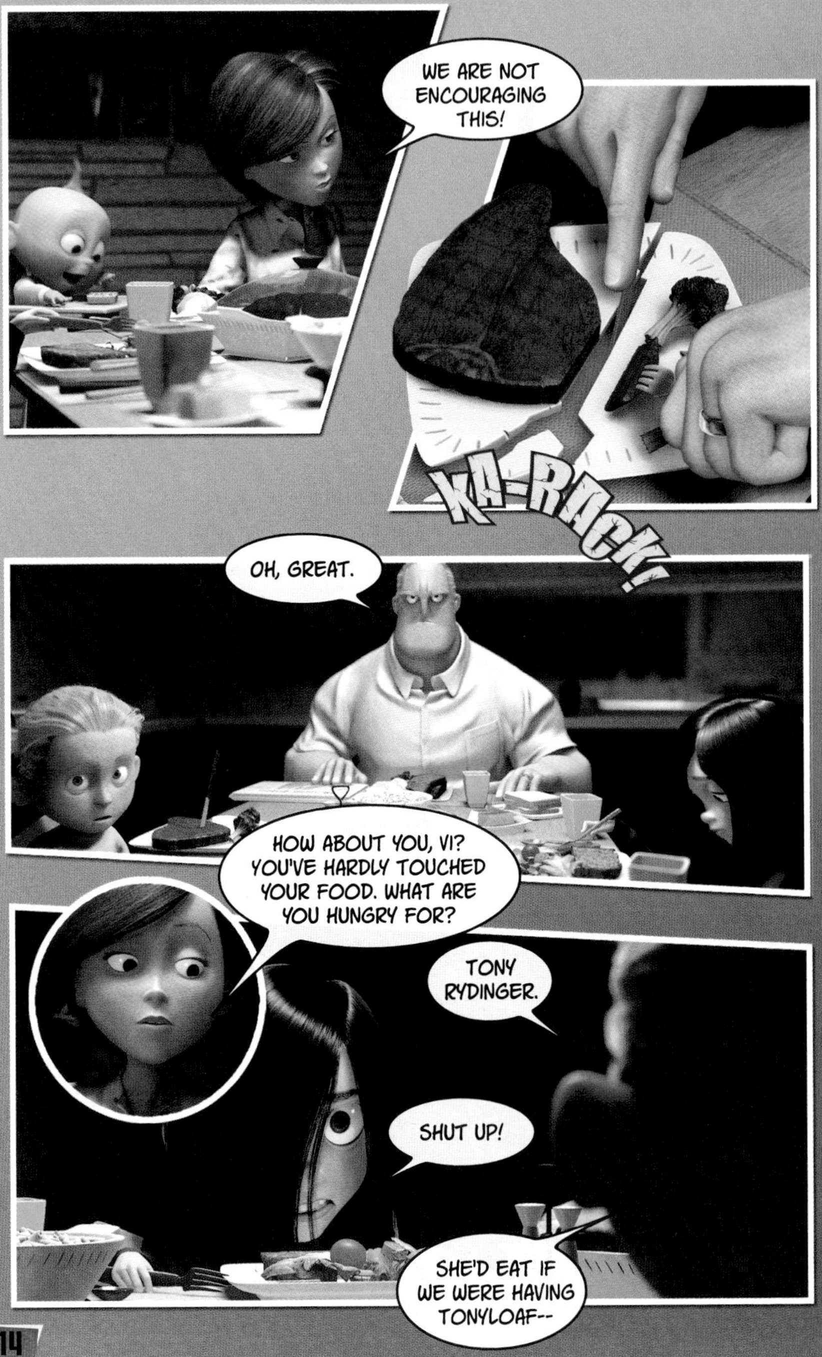
WE ARE NOT ENCOURAGING THIS!
KA-RACK!
OH, GREAT.
HOW ABOUT YOU, VI? YOU'VE HARDLY TOUCHED YOUR FOOD. WHAT ARE YOU HUNGRY FOR?
TONY RYDINGER.
SHUT UP!
SHE'D EAT IF WE WERE HAVING TONYLOAF--

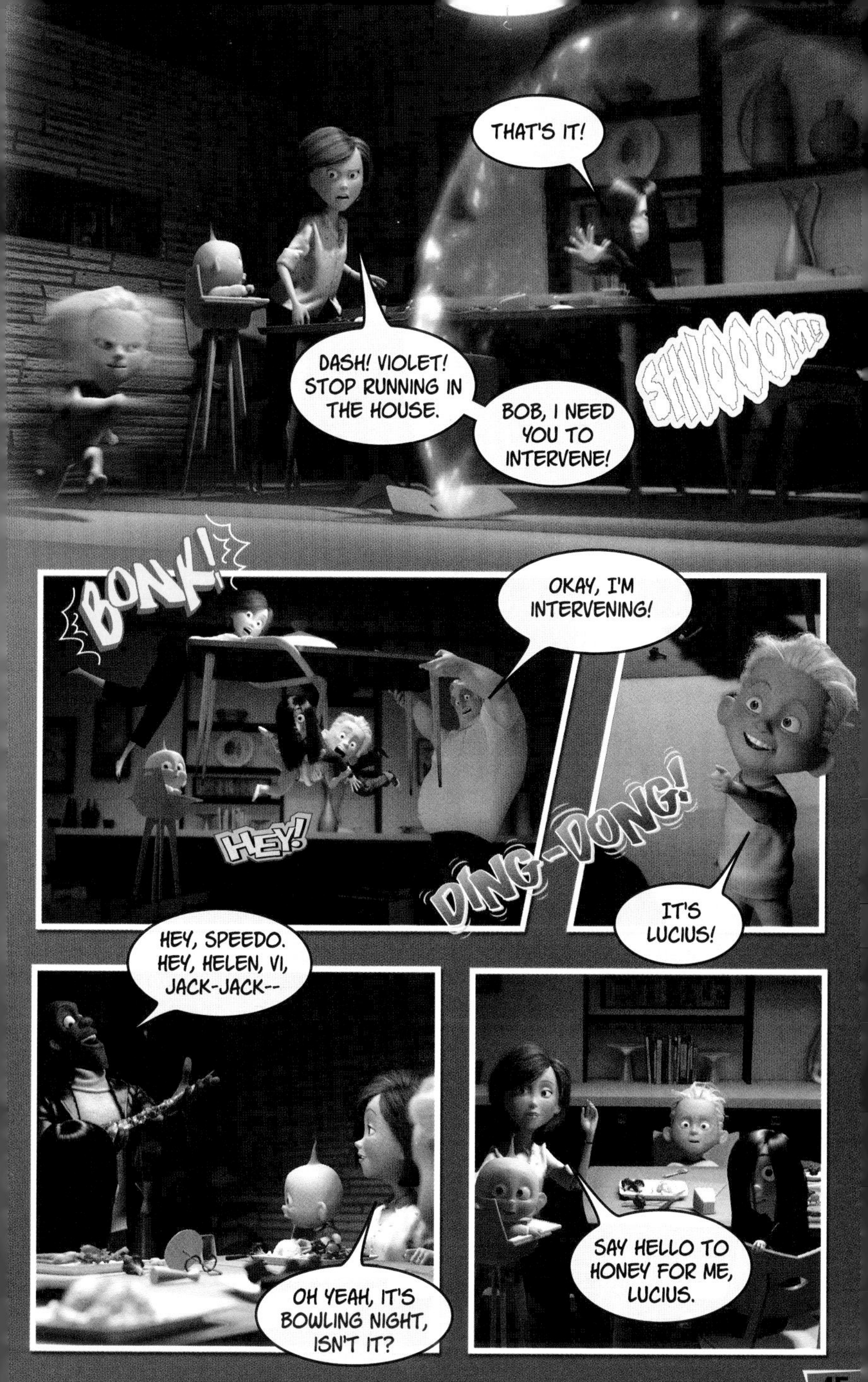
THAT'S IT!
DASH! VIOLET! STOP RUNNING IN THE HOUSE.
BOB, I NEED YOU TO INTERVENE!
SHVOOOM!
BONK!
OKAY, I'M INTERVENING!
HEY!
DING-DONG!
IT'S LUCIUS!
HEY, SPEEDO. HEY, HELEN, VI, JACK-JACK--
OH YEAH, IT'S BOWLING NIGHT, ISN'T IT?
SAY HELLO TO HONEY FOR ME, LUCIUS.

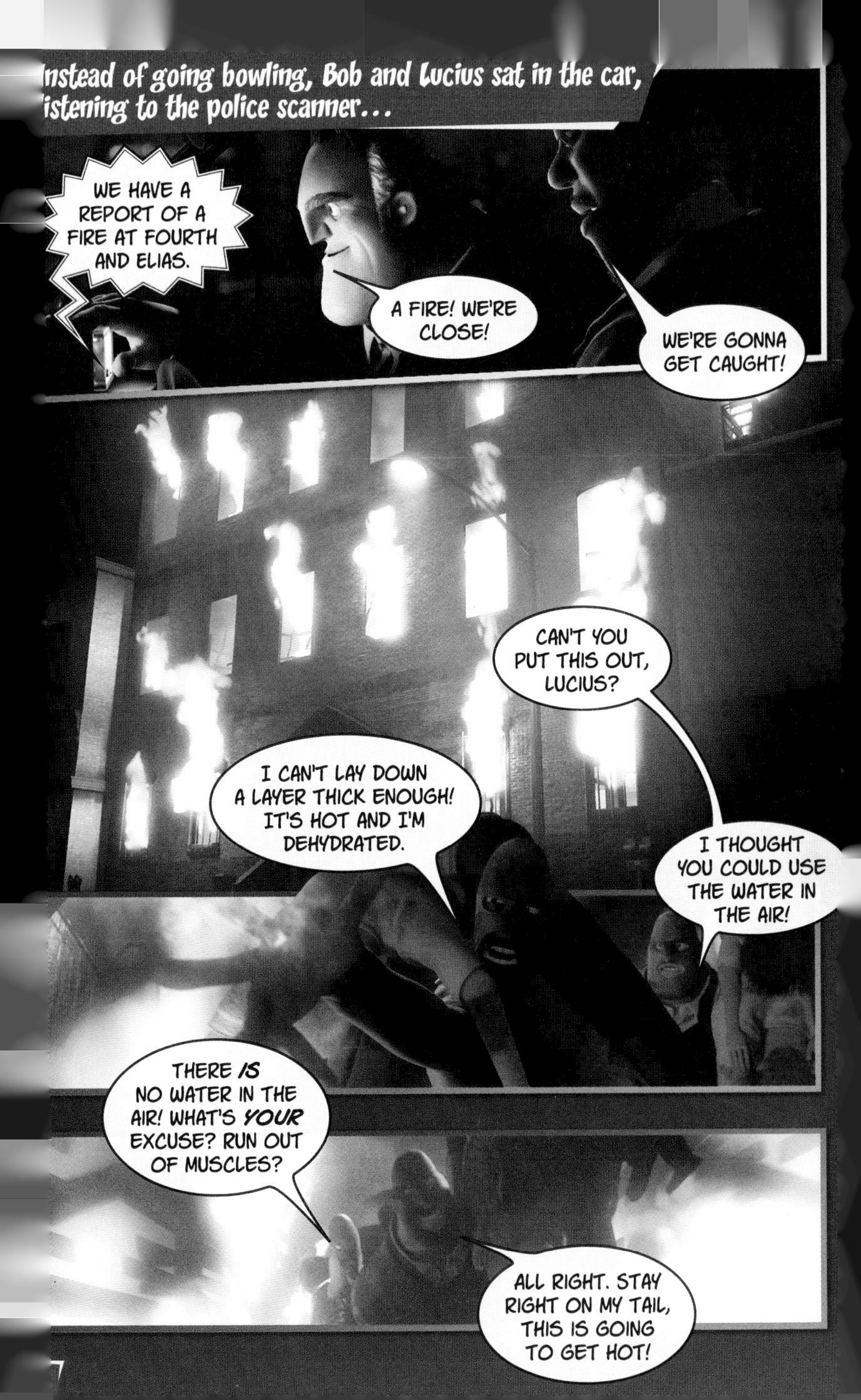
Instead of going bowling, Bob and Lucius sat in the car, listening to the police scanner...
WE HAVE A REPORT OF A FIRE AT FOURTH AND ELIAS.
A FIRE! WE'RE CLOSE!
WE'RE GONNA GET CAUGHT!
CAN'T YOU PUT THIS OUT, LUCIUS?
I CAN'T LAY DOWN A LAYER THICK ENOUGH! IT'S HOT AND I'M DEHYDRATED.
I THOUGHT YOU COULD USE THE WATER IN THE AIR!
THERE IS NO WATER IN THE AIR! WHAT'S YOUR EXCUSE? RUN OUT OF MUSCLES?
ALL RIGHT. STAY RIGHT ON MY TAIL, THIS IS GOING TO GET HOT!

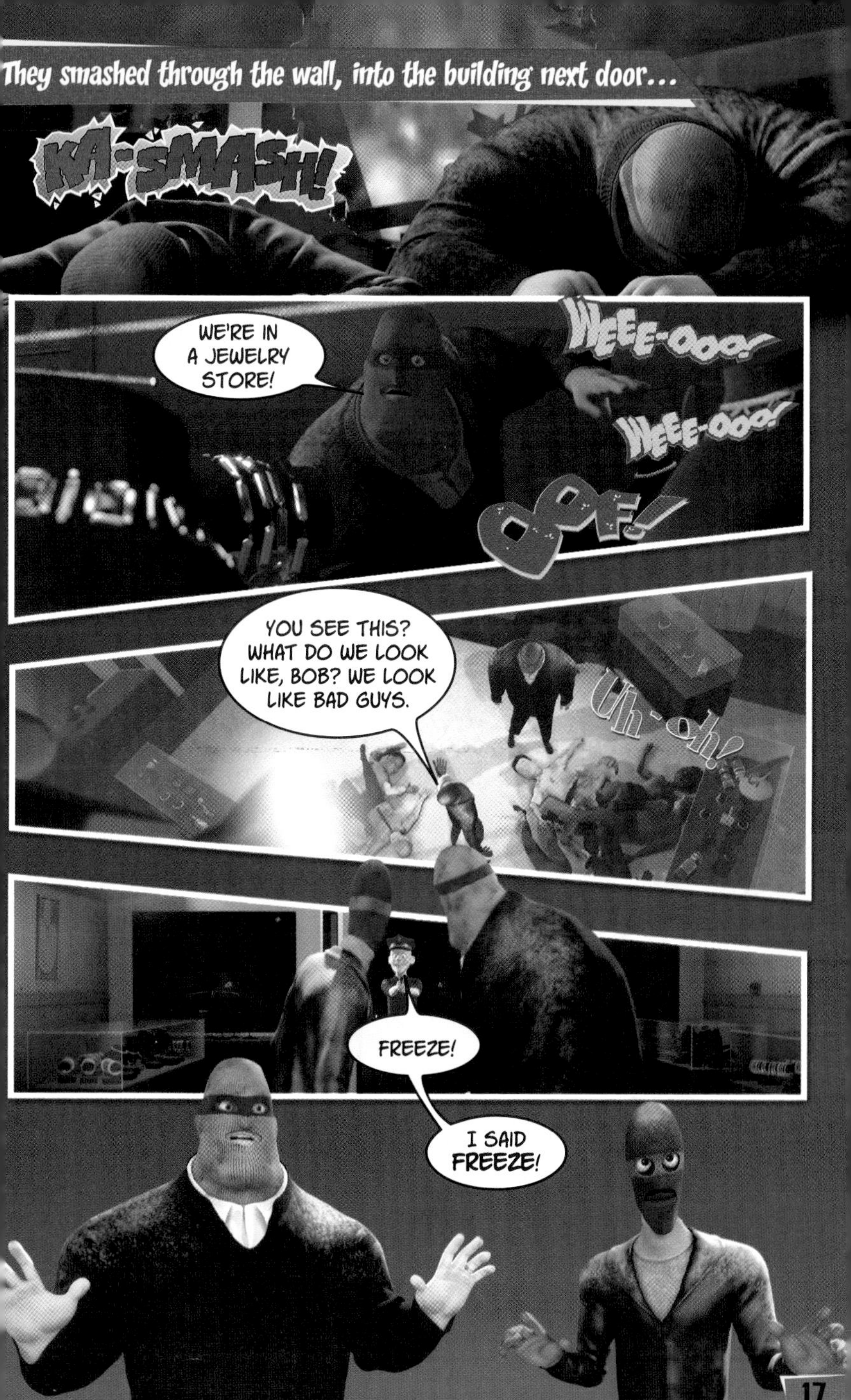
They smashed through the wall, into the building next door...
KA-SMASH!
WE'RE IN A JEWELRY STORE!
WEEE-OOO!
WEEE-OOO!
OOF!
YOU SEE THIS? WHAT DO WE LOOK LIKE, BOB? WE LOOK LIKE BAD GUYS.
Uh-oh!
FREEZE!
I SAID FREEZE!

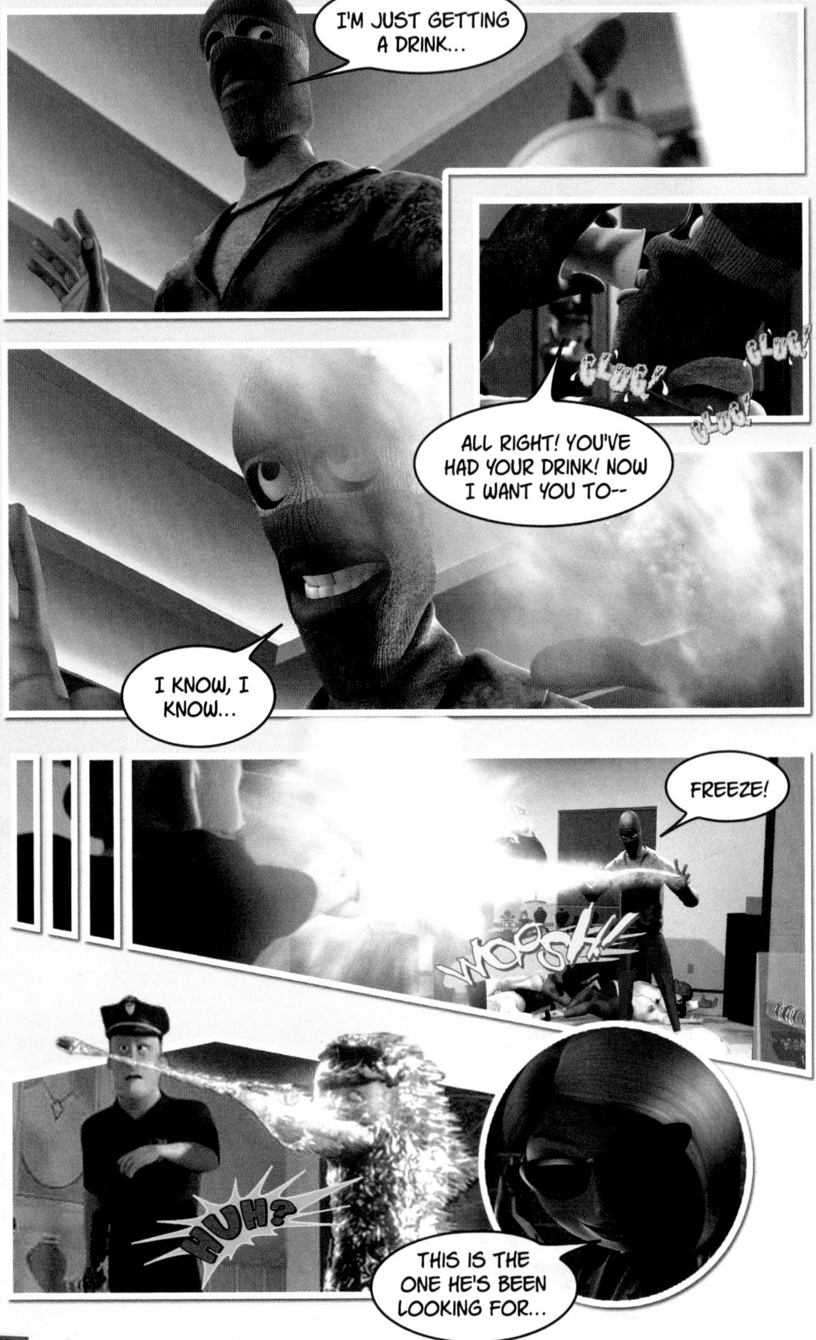

I'M JUST GETTING A DRINK...
GLUG! GLUG! GLUG!
ALL RIGHT! YOU'VE HAD YOUR DRINK! NOW I WANT YOU TO--
I KNOW, I KNOW...
FREEZE!
WOOSH!!
HUH?
THIS IS THE ONE HE'S BEEN LOOKING FOR...

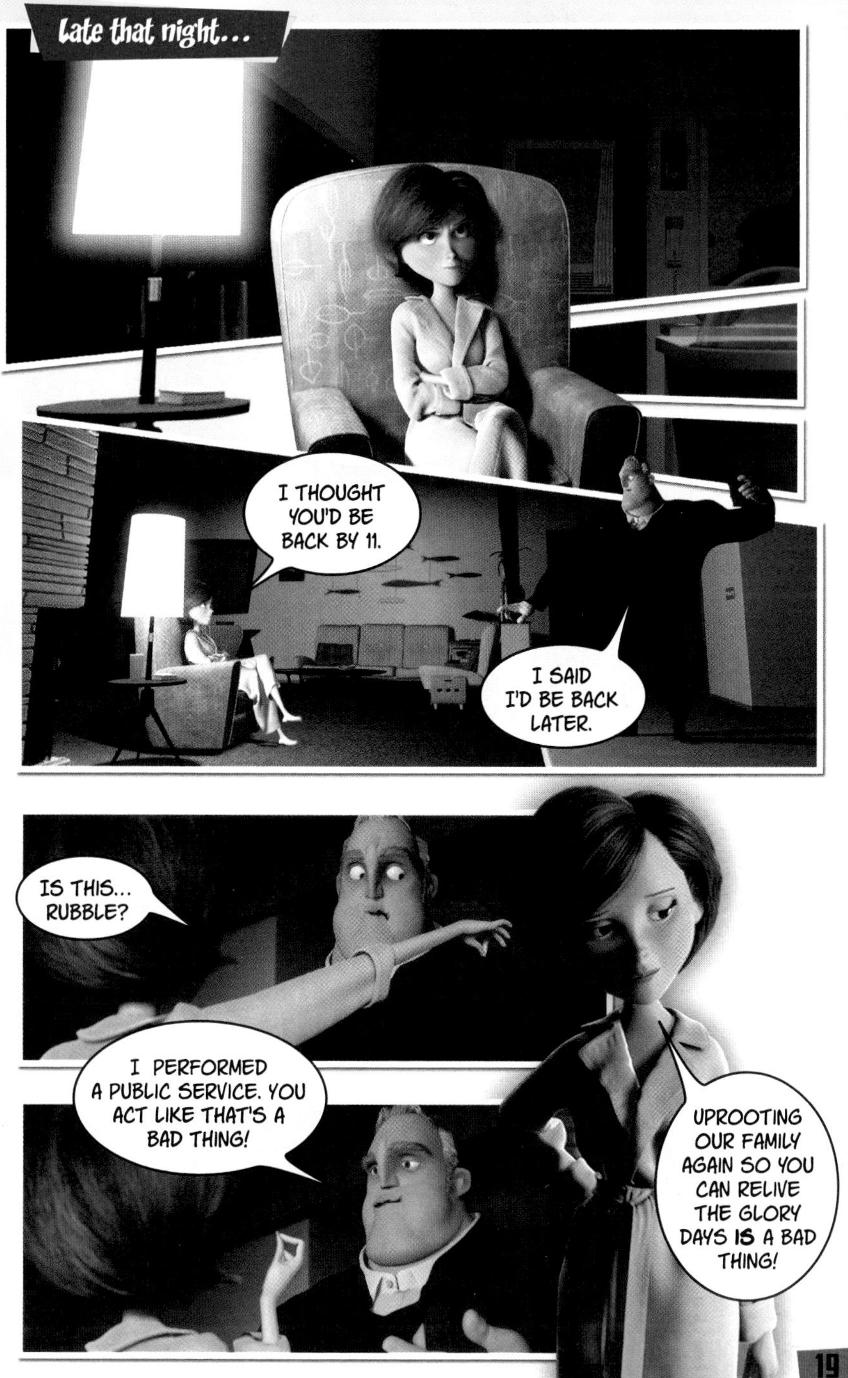
Late that night...
I THOUGHT YOU'D BE BACK BY 11.
I SAID I'D BE BACK LATER.
IS THIS... RUBBLE?
I PERFORMED A PUBLIC SERVICE. YOU ACT LIKE THAT'S A BAD THING!
UPROOTING OUR FAMILY AGAIN SO YOU CAN RELIVE THE GLORY DAYS **IS** A BAD THING!

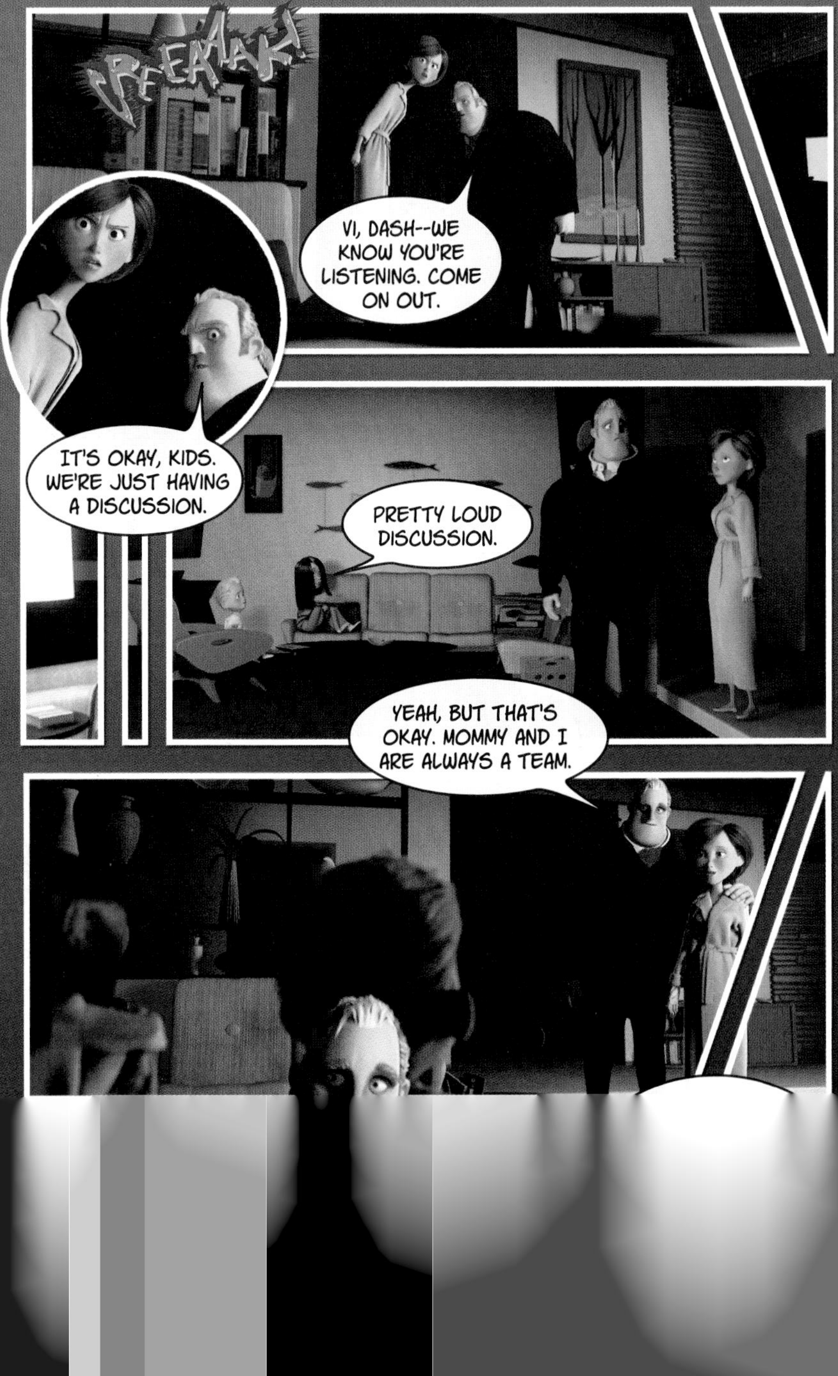

VI, DASH--WE KNOW YOU'RE LISTENING. COME ON OUT.
IT'S OKAY, KIDS. WE'RE JUST HAVING A DISCUSSION.
PRETTY LOUD DISCUSSION.
YEAH, BUT THAT'S OKAY. MOMMY AND I ARE ALWAYS A TEAM.

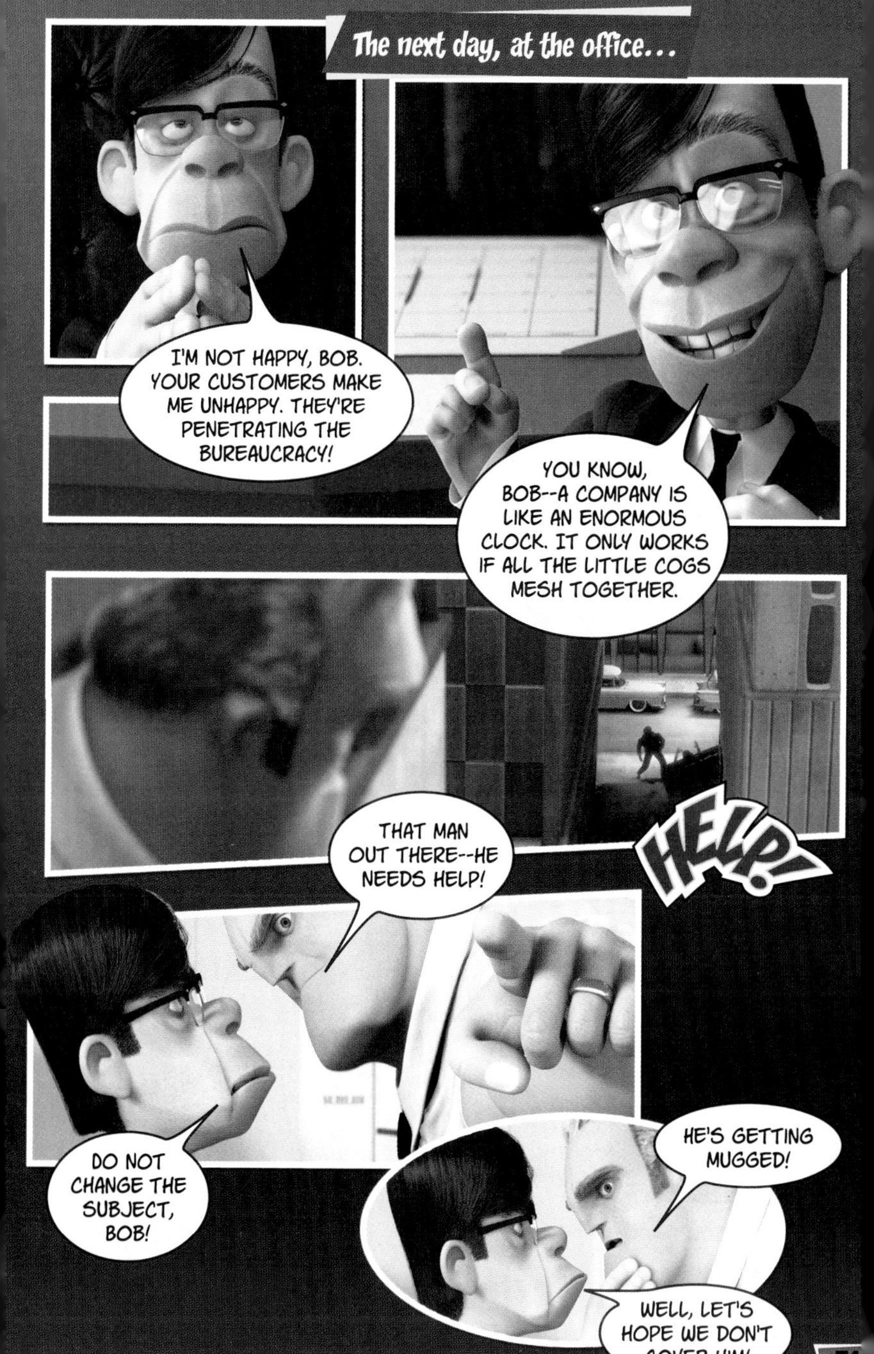

The next day, at the office...
I'M NOT HAPPY, BOB. YOUR CUSTOMERS MAKE ME UNHAPPY. THEY'RE PENETRATING THE BUREAUCRACY!
YOU KNOW, BOB--A COMPANY IS LIKE AN ENORMOUS CLOCK. IT ONLY WORKS IF ALL THE LITTLE COGS MESH TOGETHER.
HELP!
THAT MAN OUT THERE--HE NEEDS HELP!
DO NOT CHANGE THE SUBJECT, BOB!
HE'S GETTING MUGGED!
WELL, LET'S HOPE WE DON'T COVER HIM!

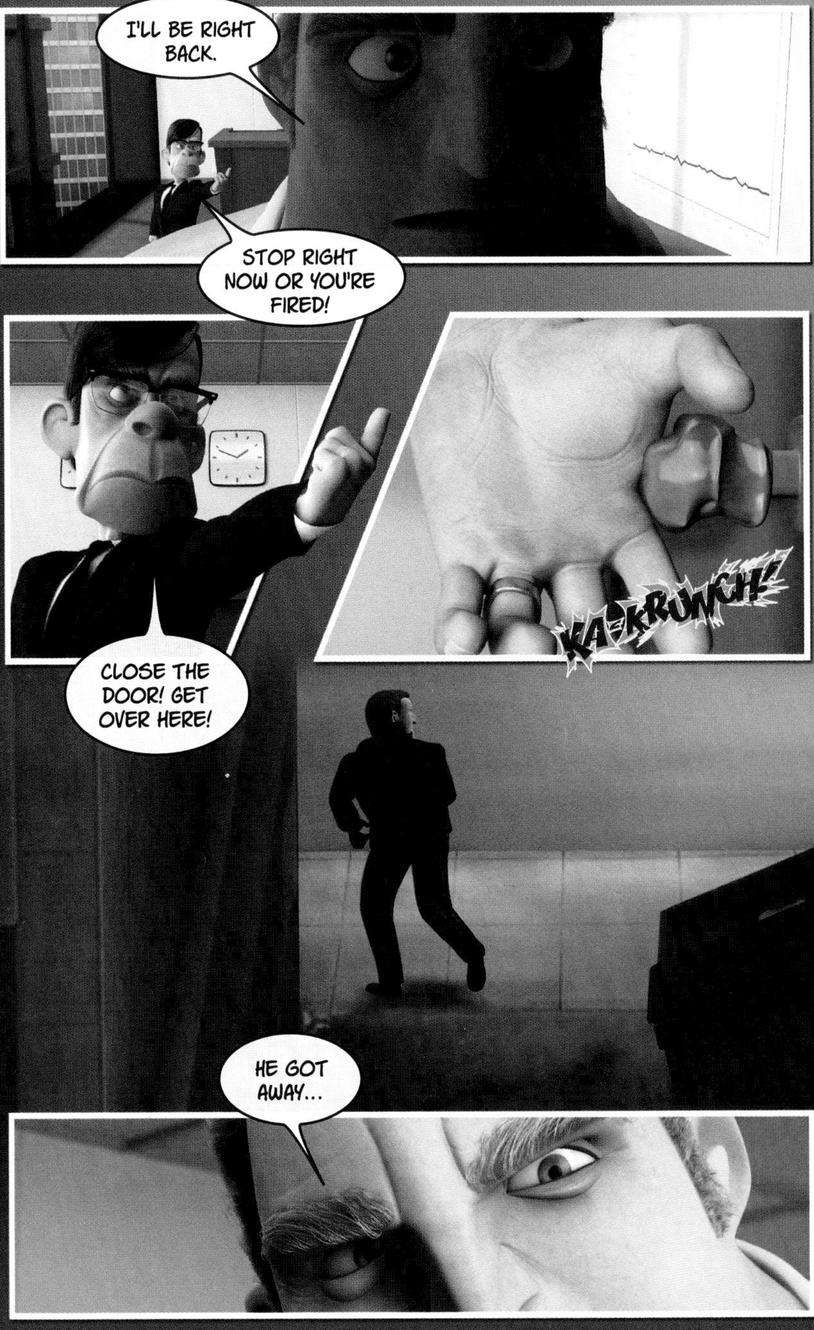
I'LL BE RIGHT BACK.
STOP RIGHT NOW OR YOU'RE FIRED!
CLOSE THE DOOR! GET OVER HERE!
KA-KRUNCH!
HE GOT AWAY...

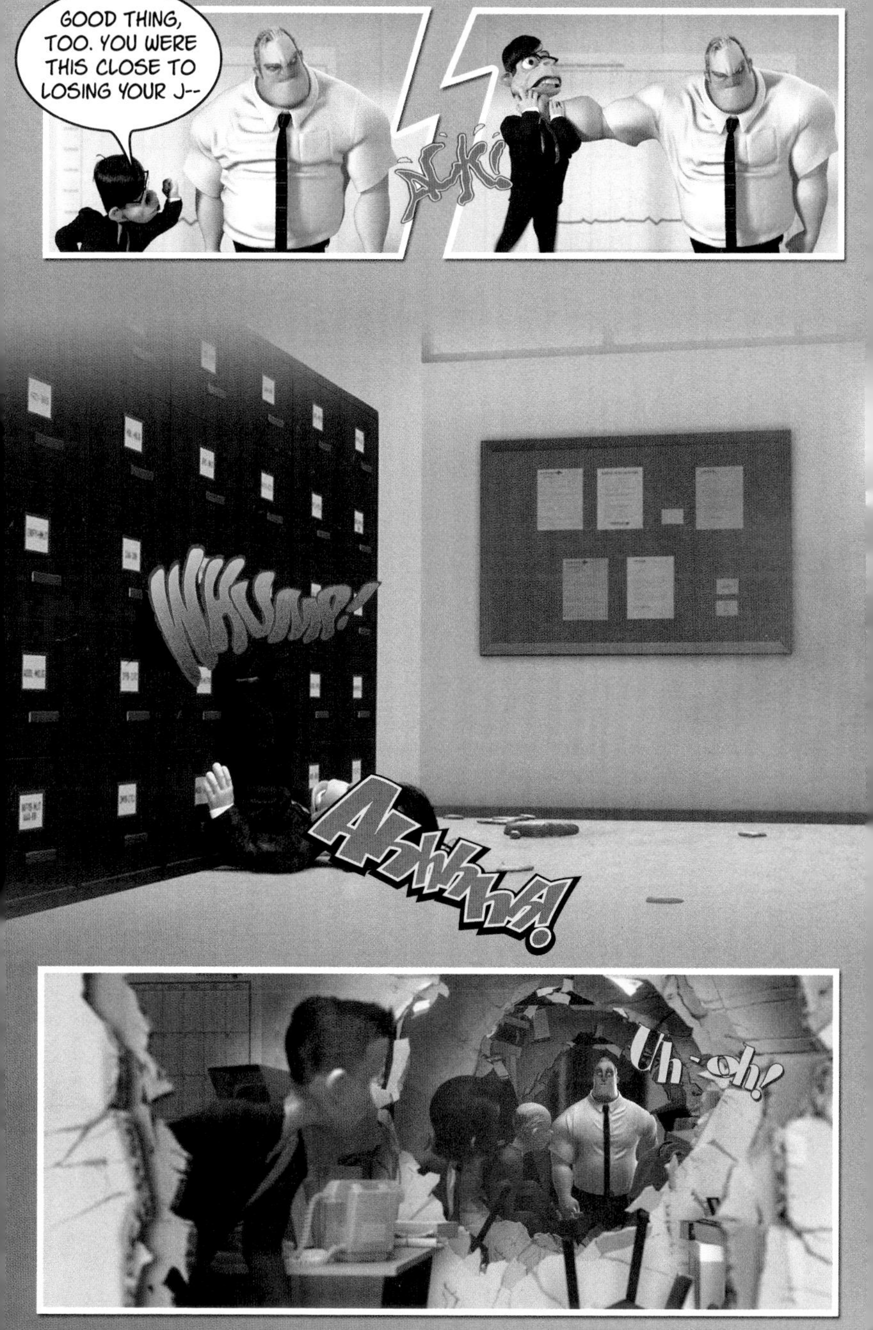
GOOD THING, TOO. YOU WERE THIS CLOSE TO LOSING YOUR J--
ACK!
WHUMP!
AHHHH!
Uh-oh!

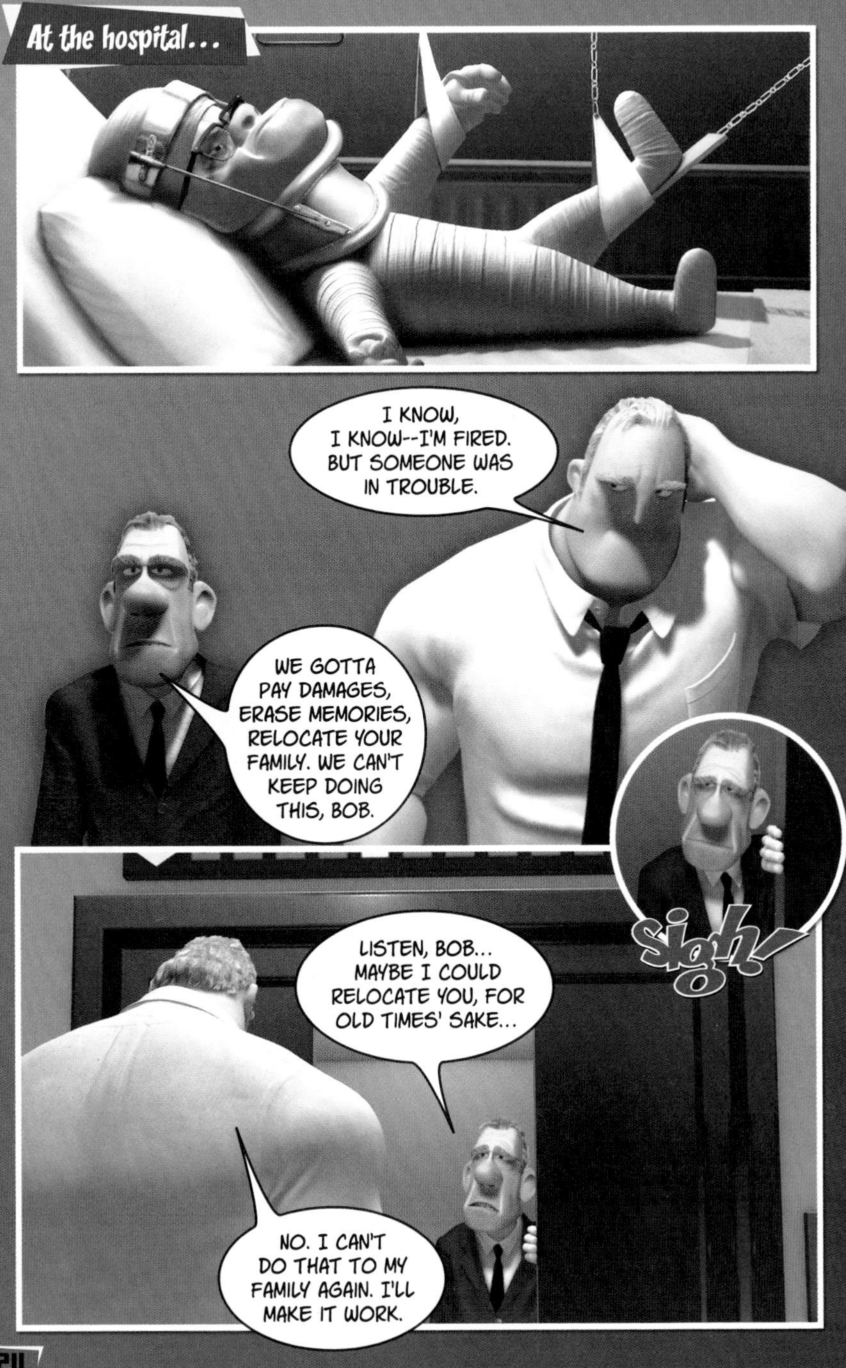
At the hospital...
I KNOW, I KNOW--I'M FIRED. BUT SOMEONE WAS IN TROUBLE.
WE GOTTA PAY DAMAGES, ERASE MEMORIES, RELOCATE YOUR FAMILY. WE CAN'T KEEP DOING THIS, BOB.
sigh!
LISTEN, BOB... MAYBE I COULD RELOCATE YOU, FOR OLD TIMES' SAKE...
NO. I CAN'T DO THAT TO MY FAMILY AGAIN. I'LL MAKE IT WORK.

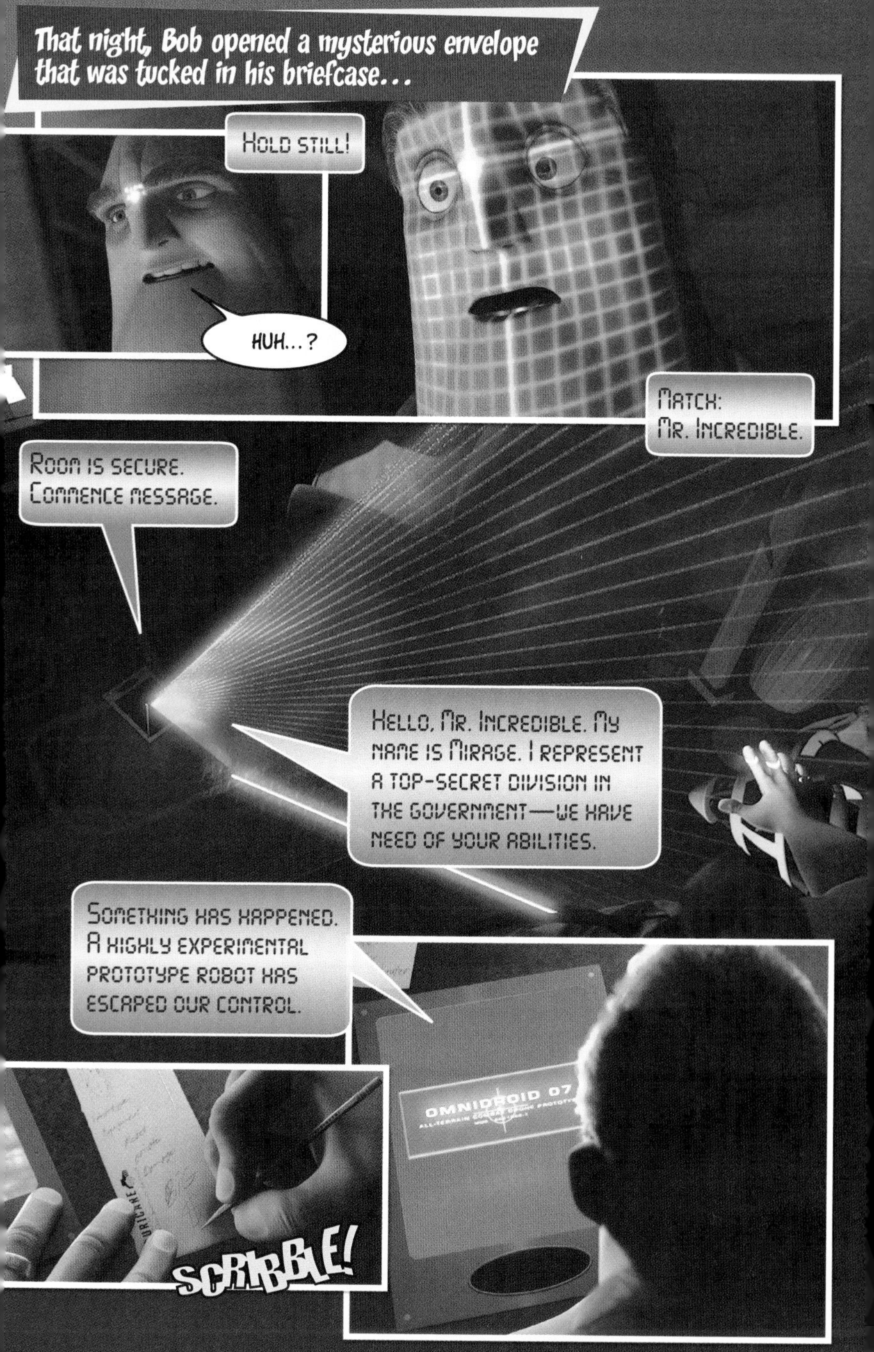

That night, Bob opened a mysterious envelope that was tucked in his briefcase...
Hold still!
Huh...?
Match: Mr. Incredible.
Room is secure. Commence message.
Hello, Mr. Incredible. My name is Mirage. I represent a top-secret division in the government—we have need of your abilities.
Something has happened. A highly experimental prototype robot has escaped our control.
OMNIDROID 07
SCRIBBLE!

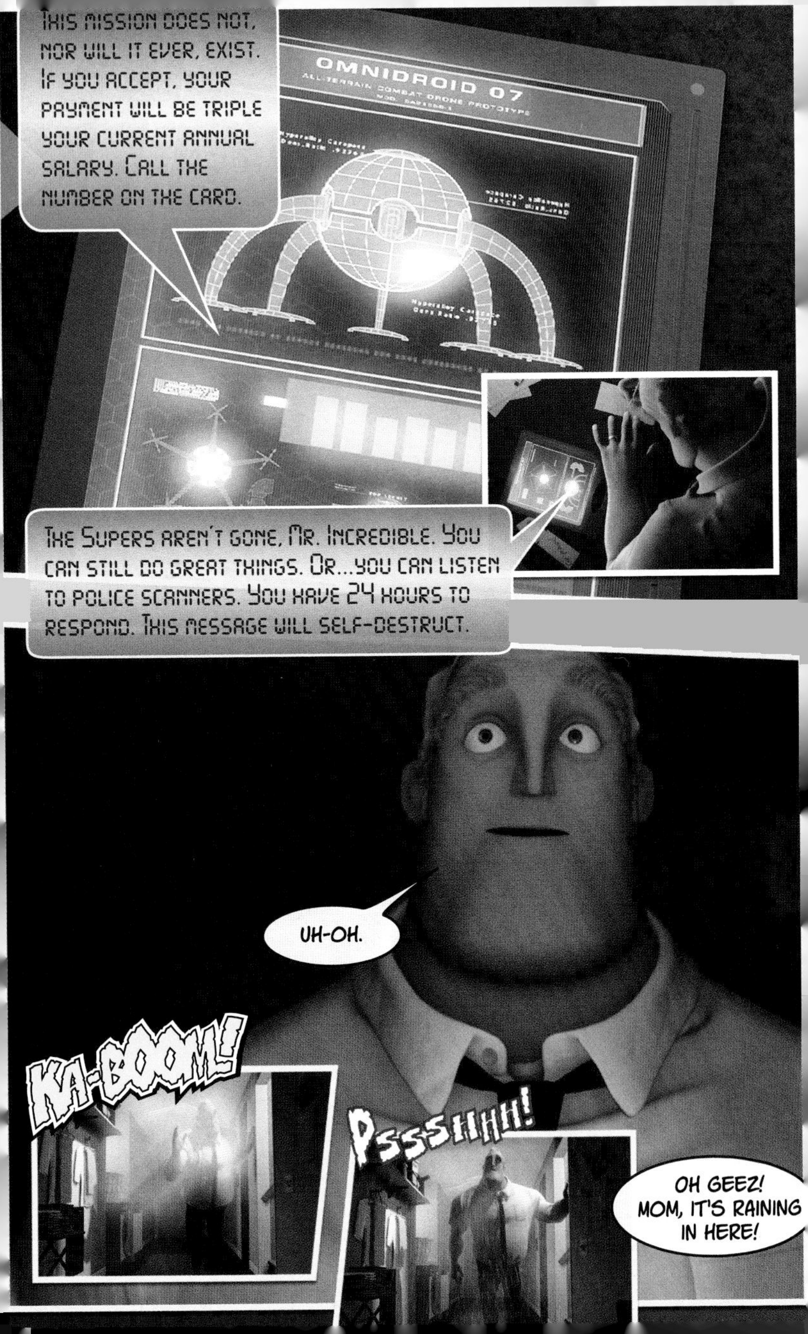
OMNIDROID 07
ALL-TERRAIN COMBAT DRONE PROTOTYPE
THIS MISSION DOES NOT, NOR WILL IT EVER, EXIST. IF YOU ACCEPT, YOUR PAYMENT WILL BE TRIPLE YOUR CURRENT ANNUAL SALARY. CALL THE NUMBER ON THE CARD.
THE SUPERS AREN'T GONE, MR. INCREDIBLE. YOU CAN STILL DO GREAT THINGS. OR...YOU CAN LISTEN TO POLICE SCANNERS. YOU HAVE 24 HOURS TO RESPOND. THIS MESSAGE WILL SELF-DESTRUCT.
UH-OH.
KA-BOOM!
PSSSHHH!
OH GEEZ! MOM, IT'S RAINING IN HERE!

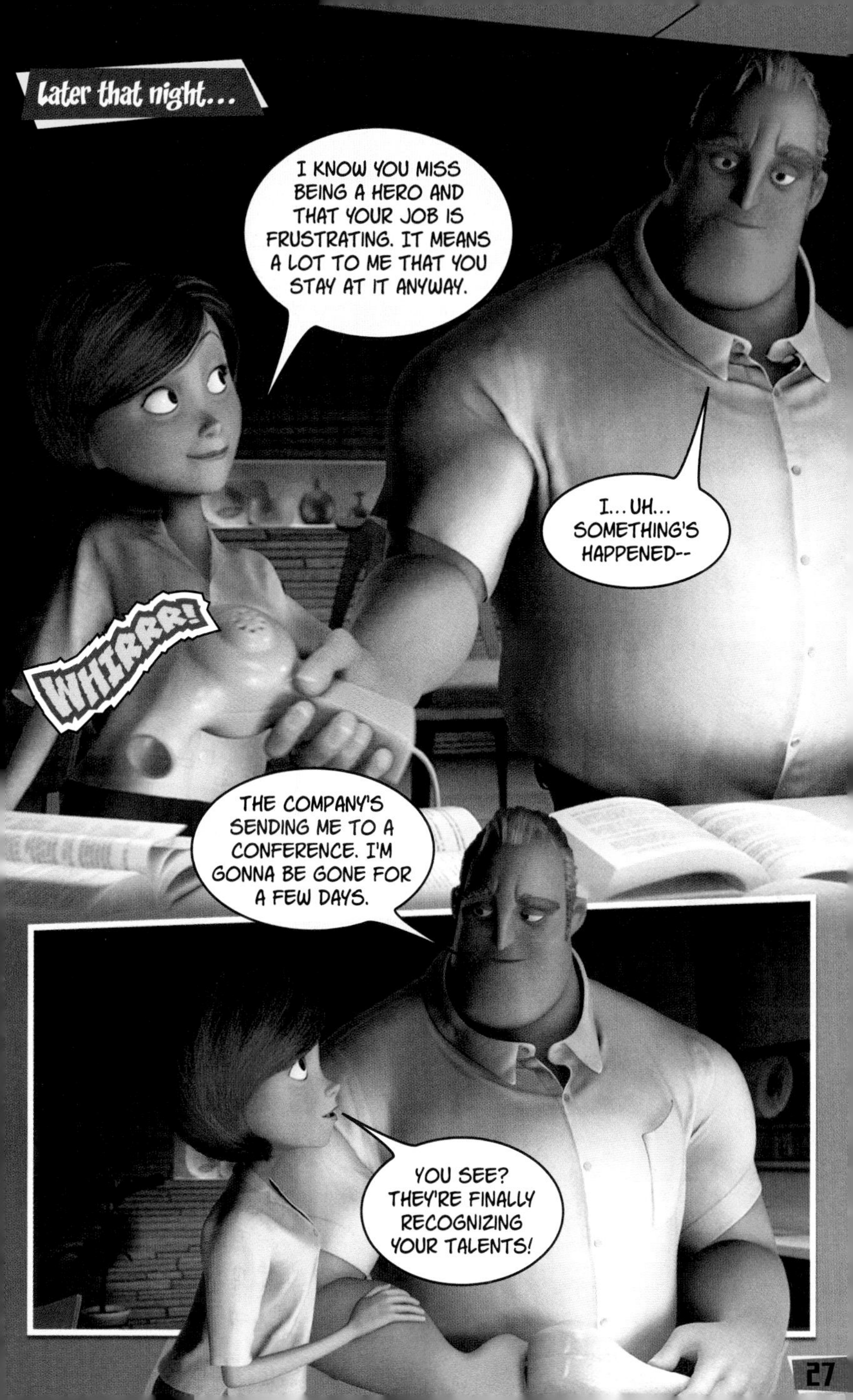
Later that night...
I KNOW YOU MISS BEING A HERO AND THAT YOUR JOB IS FRUSTRATING. IT MEANS A LOT TO ME THAT YOU STAY AT IT ANYWAY.
I... UH... SOMETHING'S HAPPENED--
WHIRRR!
THE COMPANY'S SENDING ME TO A CONFERENCE. I'M GONNA BE GONE FOR A FEW DAYS.
YOU SEE? THEY'RE FINALLY RECOGNIZING YOUR TALENTS!

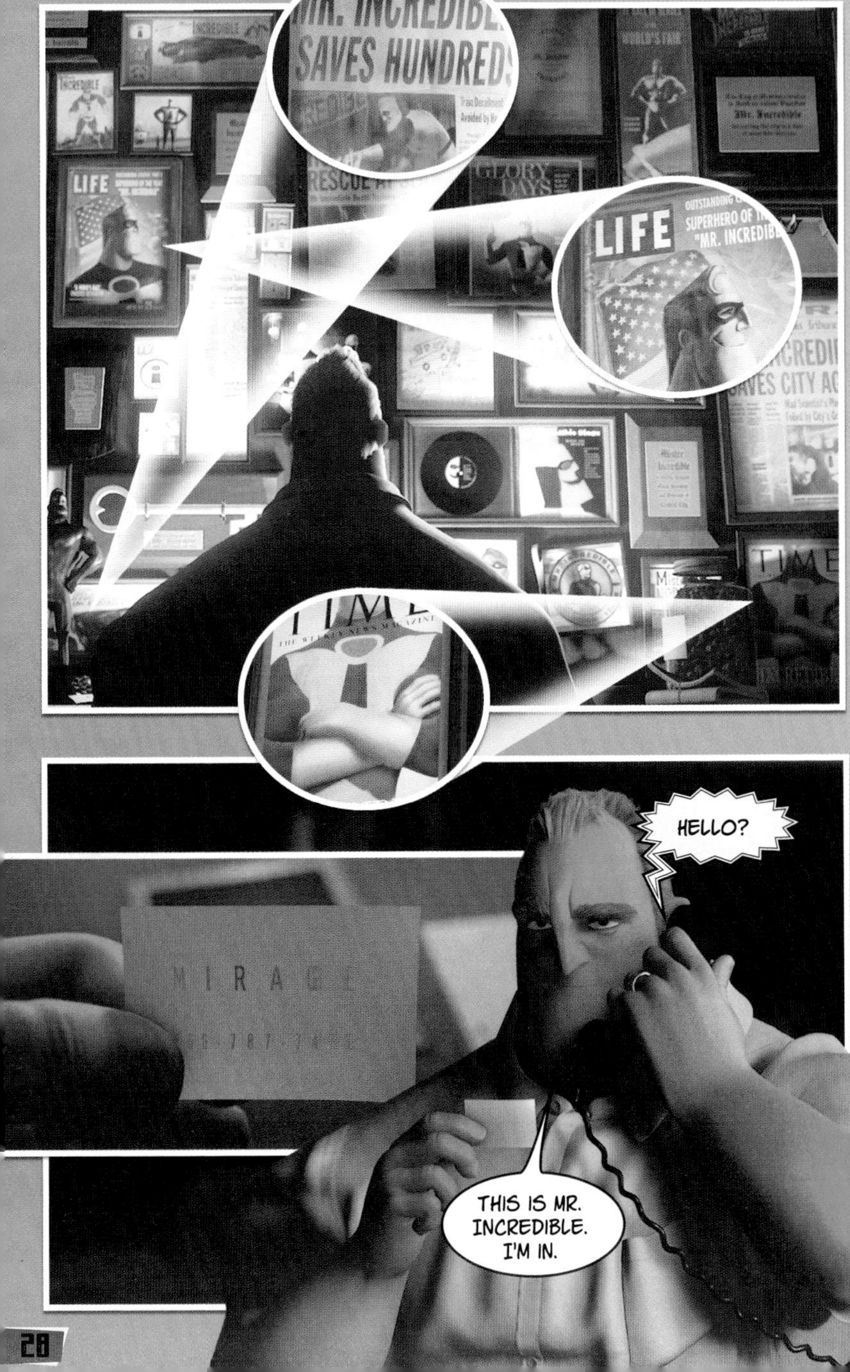
LIFE
GLORY DAYS
HELLO?
THIS IS MR. INCREDIBLE. I'M IN.

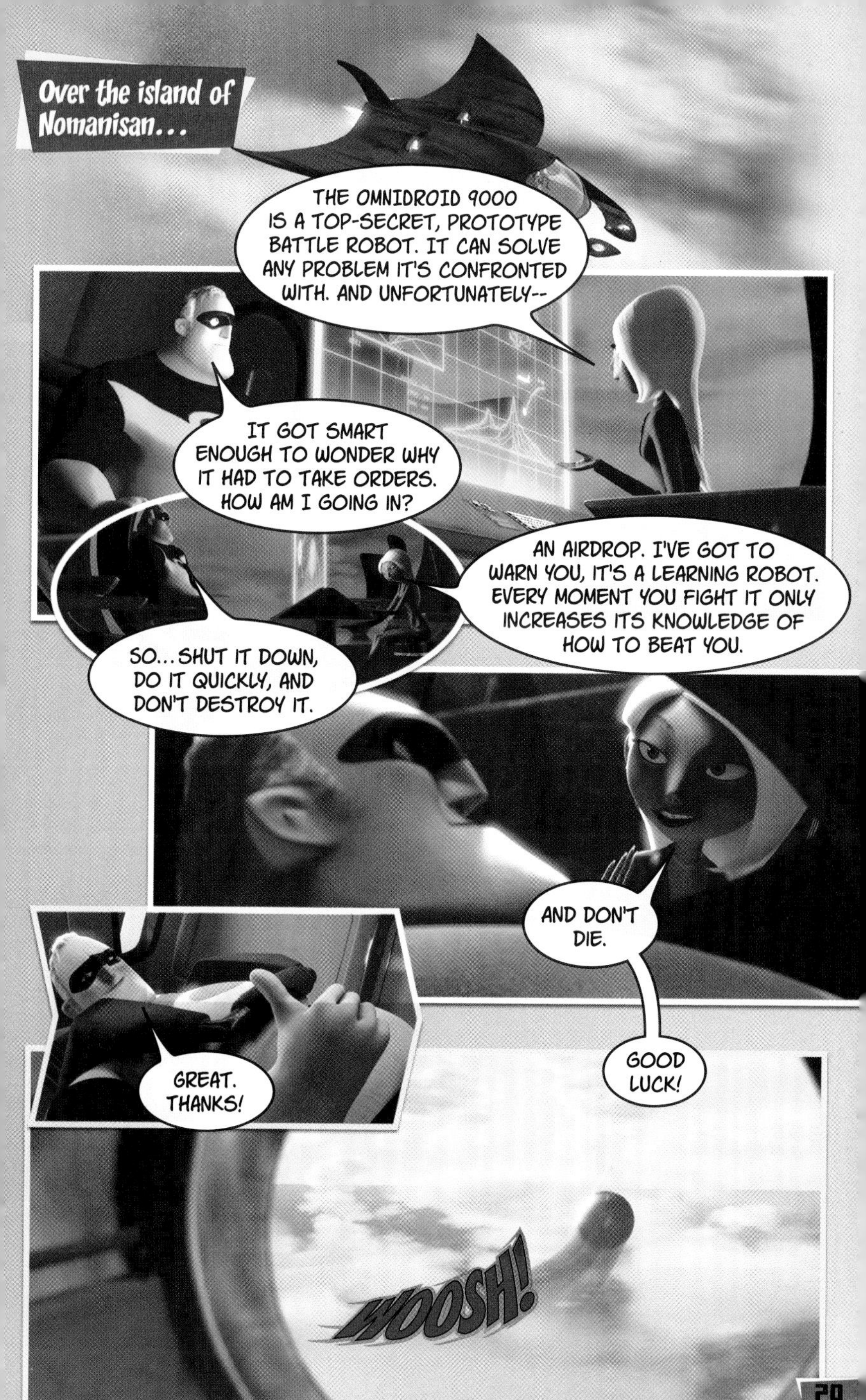
Over the island of Nomanisan...
THE OMNIDROID 9000 IS A TOP-SECRET, PROTOTYPE BATTLE ROBOT. IT CAN SOLVE ANY PROBLEM IT'S CONFRONTED WITH. AND UNFORTUNATELY--
IT GOT SMART ENOUGH TO WONDER WHY IT HAD TO TAKE ORDERS. HOW AM I GOING IN?
AN AIRDROP. I'VE GOT TO WARN YOU, IT'S A LEARNING ROBOT. EVERY MOMENT YOU FIGHT IT ONLY INCREASES ITS KNOWLEDGE OF HOW TO BEAT YOU.
SO...SHUT IT DOWN, DO IT QUICKLY, AND DON'T DESTROY IT.
AND DON'T DIE.
GOOD LUCK!
GREAT. THANKS!
WOOSH!

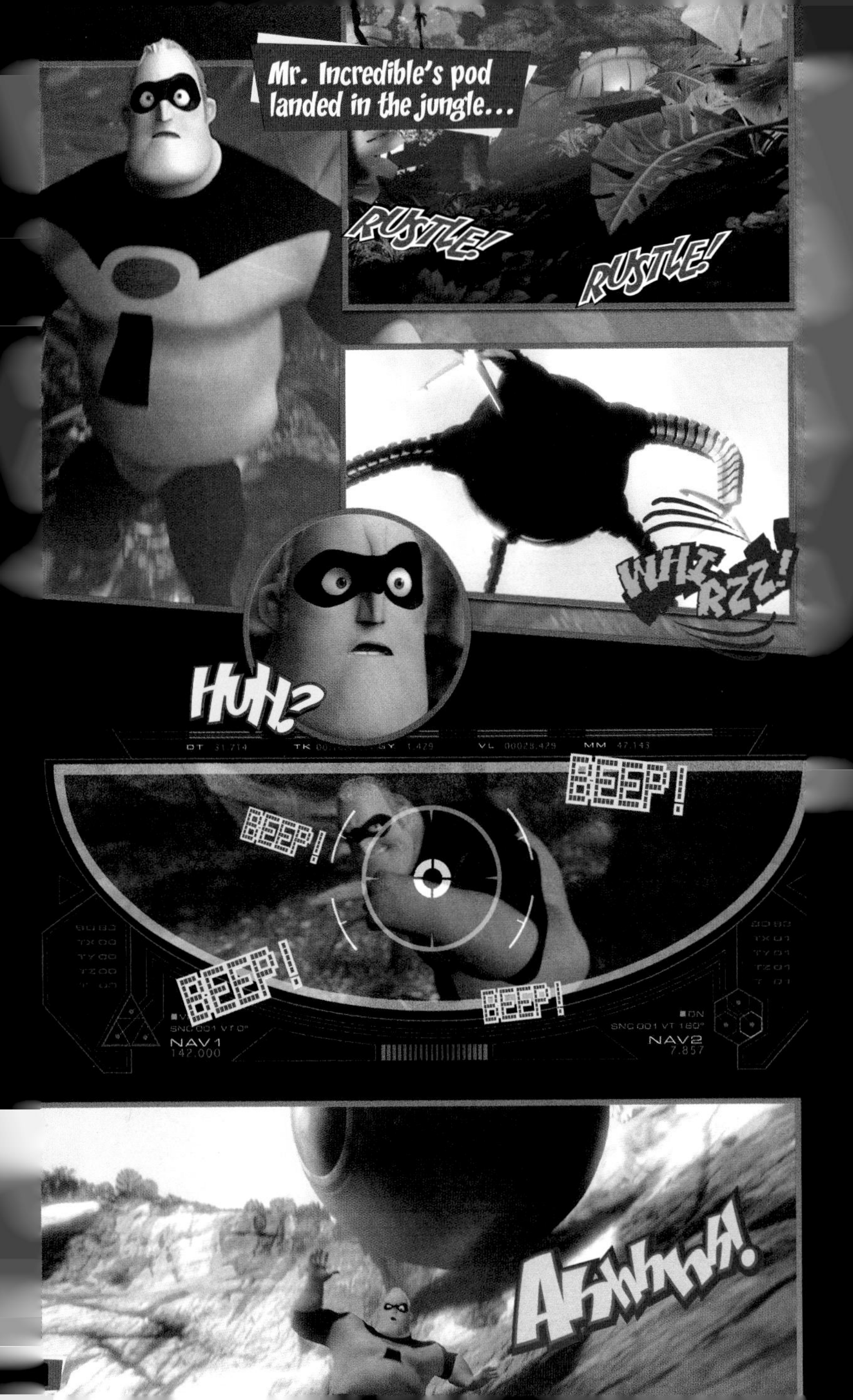
Mr. Incredible's pod landed in the jungle...
RUSTLE!
RUSTLE!
WHIRZZ!
HUH?
BEEP!
BEEP!
BEEP!
BEEP!
NAV1
142.000
NAV2
7.857
AHHHHH!

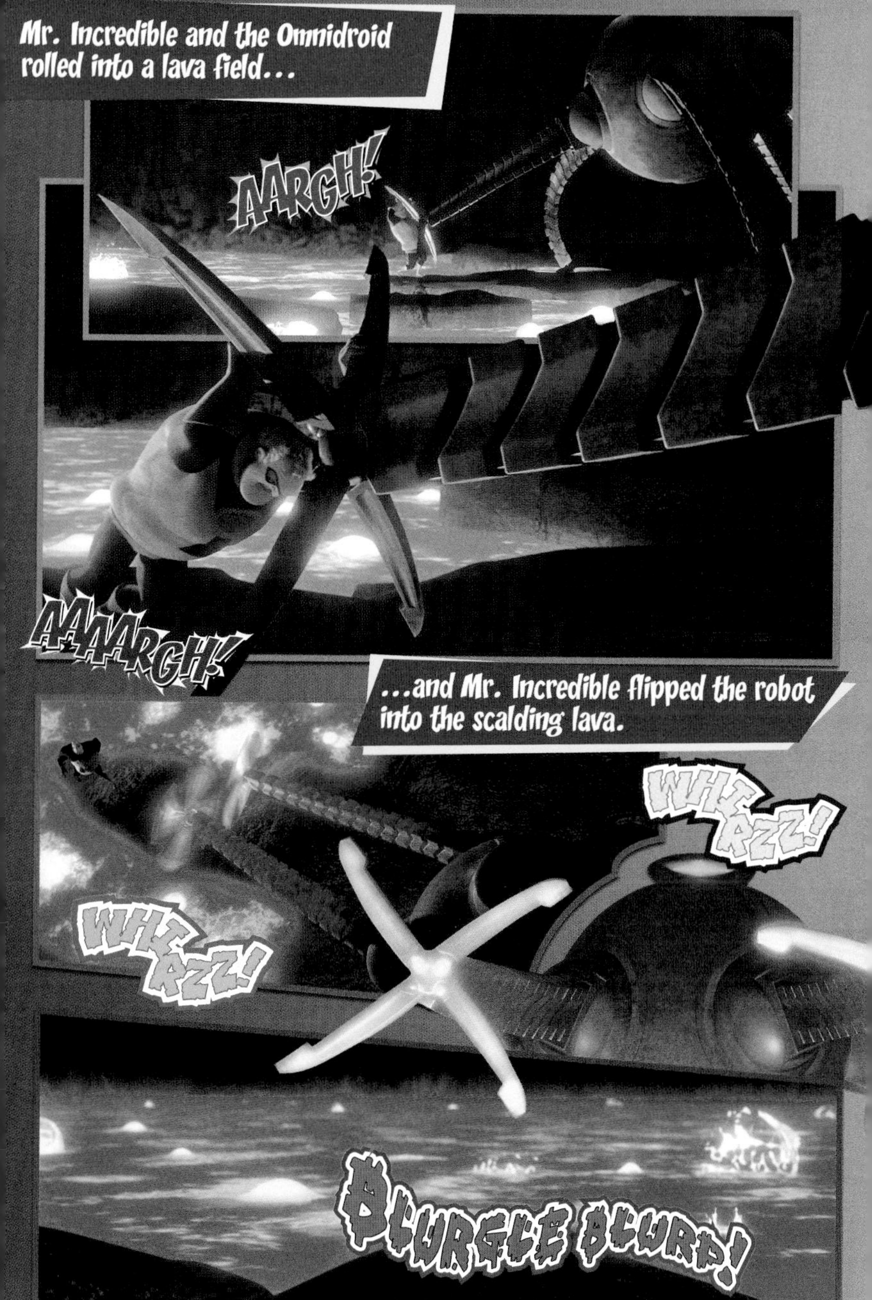
Mr. Incredible and the Omnidroid rolled into a lava field...
AARGH!
AAAARGH!
...and Mr. Incredible flipped the robot into the scalding lava.
WHIRZZ!
WHIRZZ!
BLURGLE BLURP!

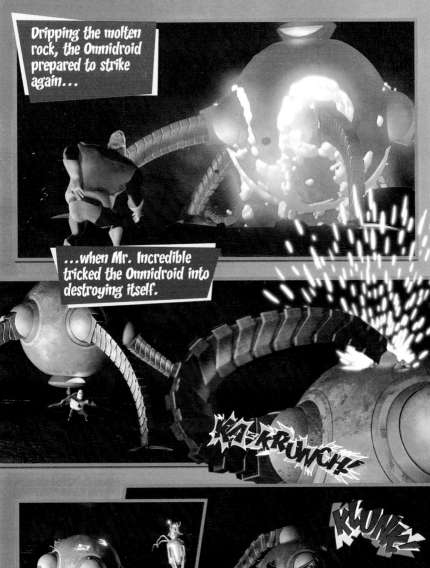

Dripping the molten rock, the Onnidroid prepared to strike again...

...when Mr. Incredible tricked the Onnidroid into destroying itself.

KA-KRUNCH!

WHIRZZ?

KLUNK!

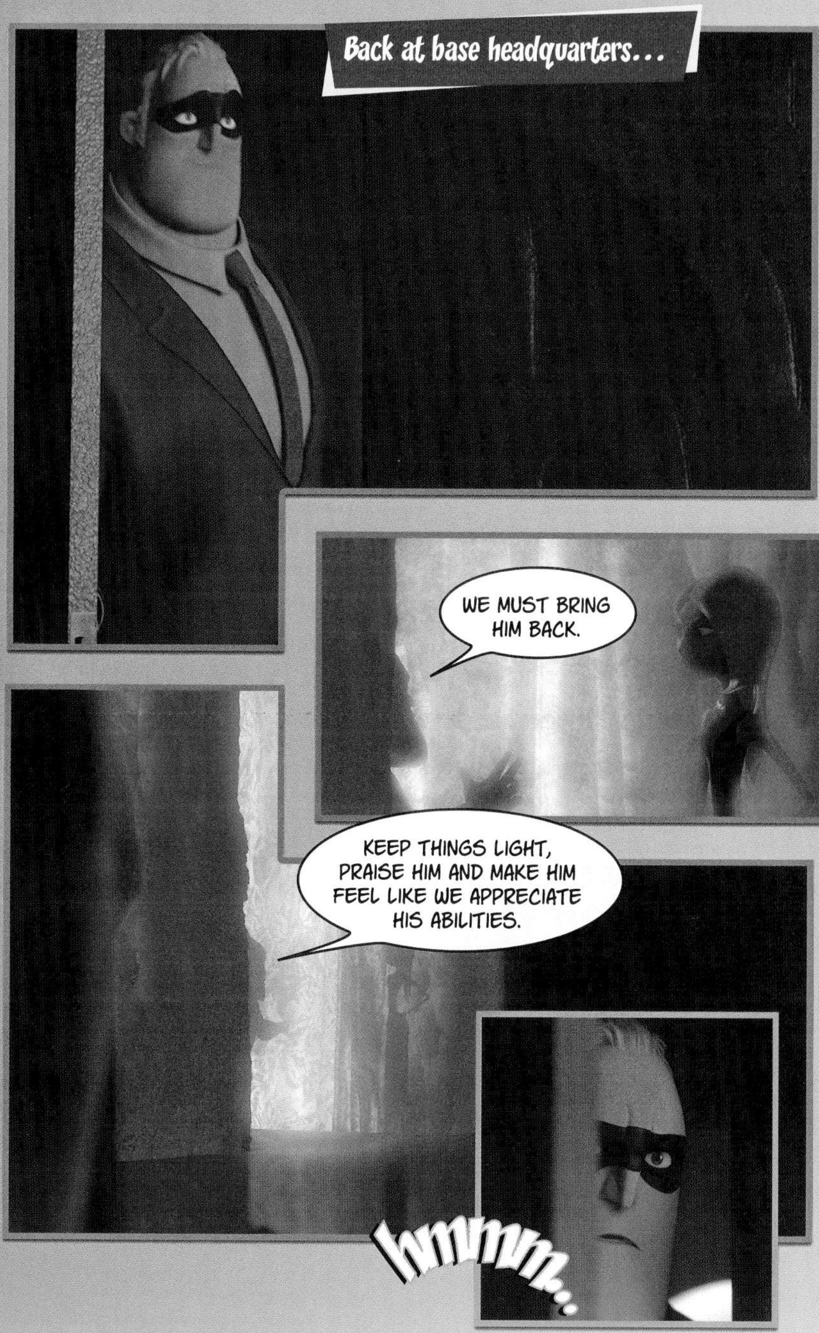
Back at base headquarters...
WE MUST BRING HIM BACK.
KEEP THINGS LIGHT, PRAISE HIM AND MAKE HIM FEEL LIKE WE APPRECIATE HIS ABILITIES.
hmmm...

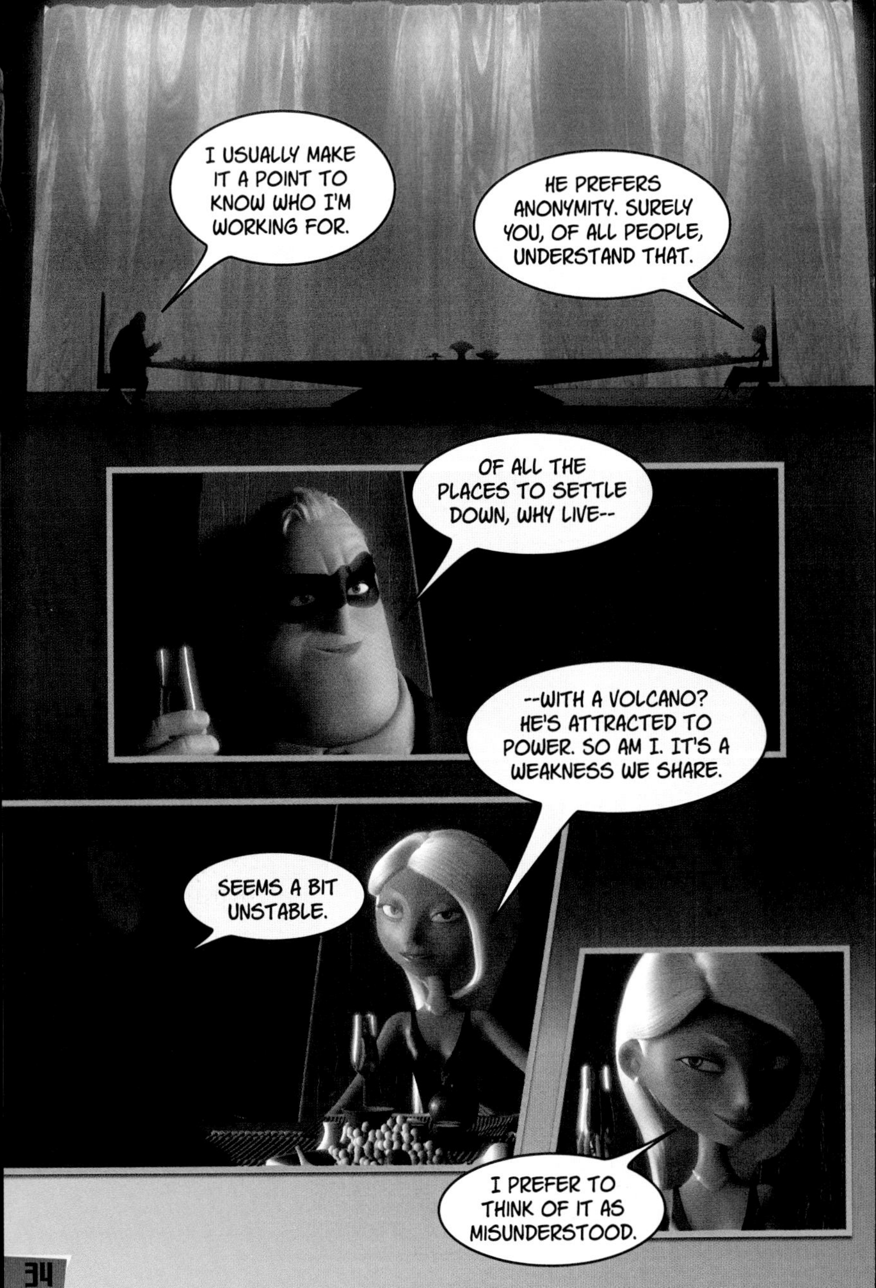
I USUALLY MAKE IT A POINT TO KNOW WHO I'M WORKING FOR.
HE PREFERS ANONYMITY. SURELY YOU, OF ALL PEOPLE, UNDERSTAND THAT.
OF ALL THE PLACES TO SETTLE DOWN, WHY LIVE--
--WITH A VOLCANO? HE'S ATTRACTED TO POWER. SO AM I. IT'S A WEAKNESS WE SHARE.
SEEMS A BIT UNSTABLE.
I PREFER TO THINK OF IT AS MISUNDERSTOOD.

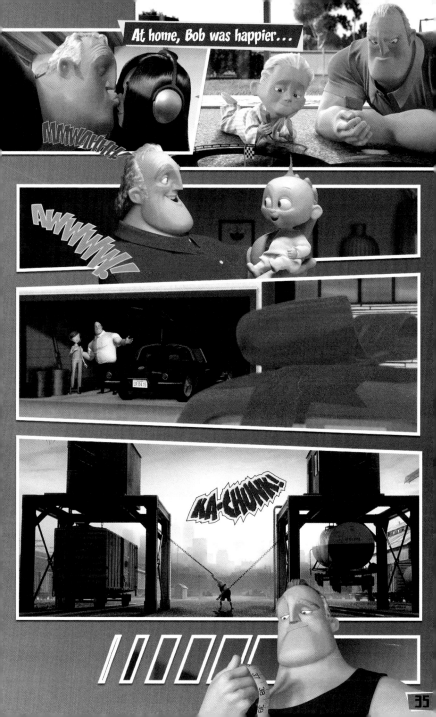

At home, Bob was happier...

MMWAHH!!!

AWWWW!!

KA-CHUNK!!

35

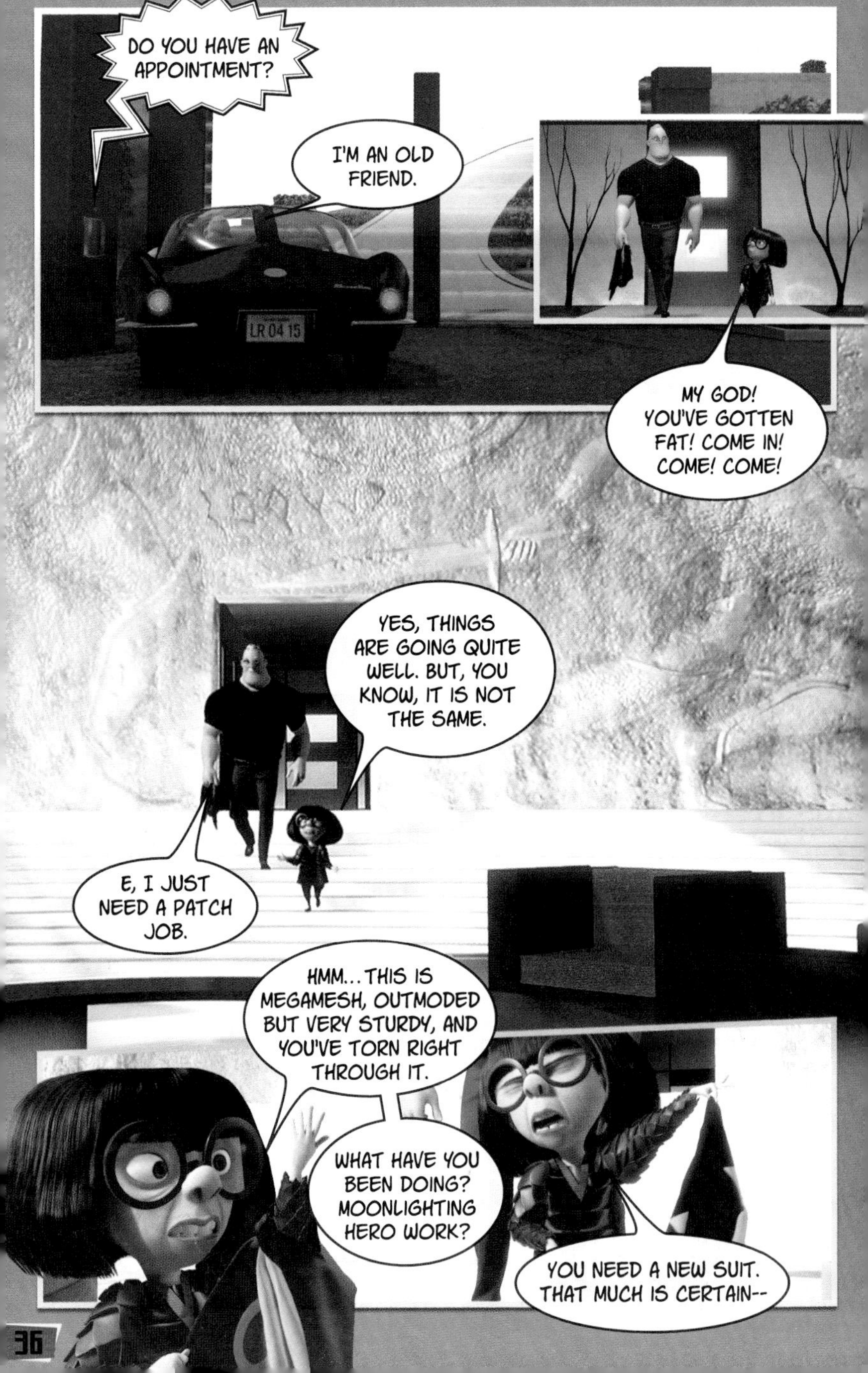
DO YOU HAVE AN APPOINTMENT?
I'M AN OLD FRIEND.
LR 04 15
MY GOD! YOU'VE GOTTEN FAT! COME IN! COME! COME!
YES, THINGS ARE GOING QUITE WELL. BUT, YOU KNOW, IT IS NOT THE SAME.
E, I JUST NEED A PATCH JOB.
HMM... THIS IS MEGAMESH, OUTMODED BUT VERY STURDY, AND YOU'VE TORN RIGHT THROUGH IT.
WHAT HAVE YOU BEEN DOING? MOONLIGHTING HERO WORK?
YOU NEED A NEW SUIT. THAT MUCH IS CERTAIN--

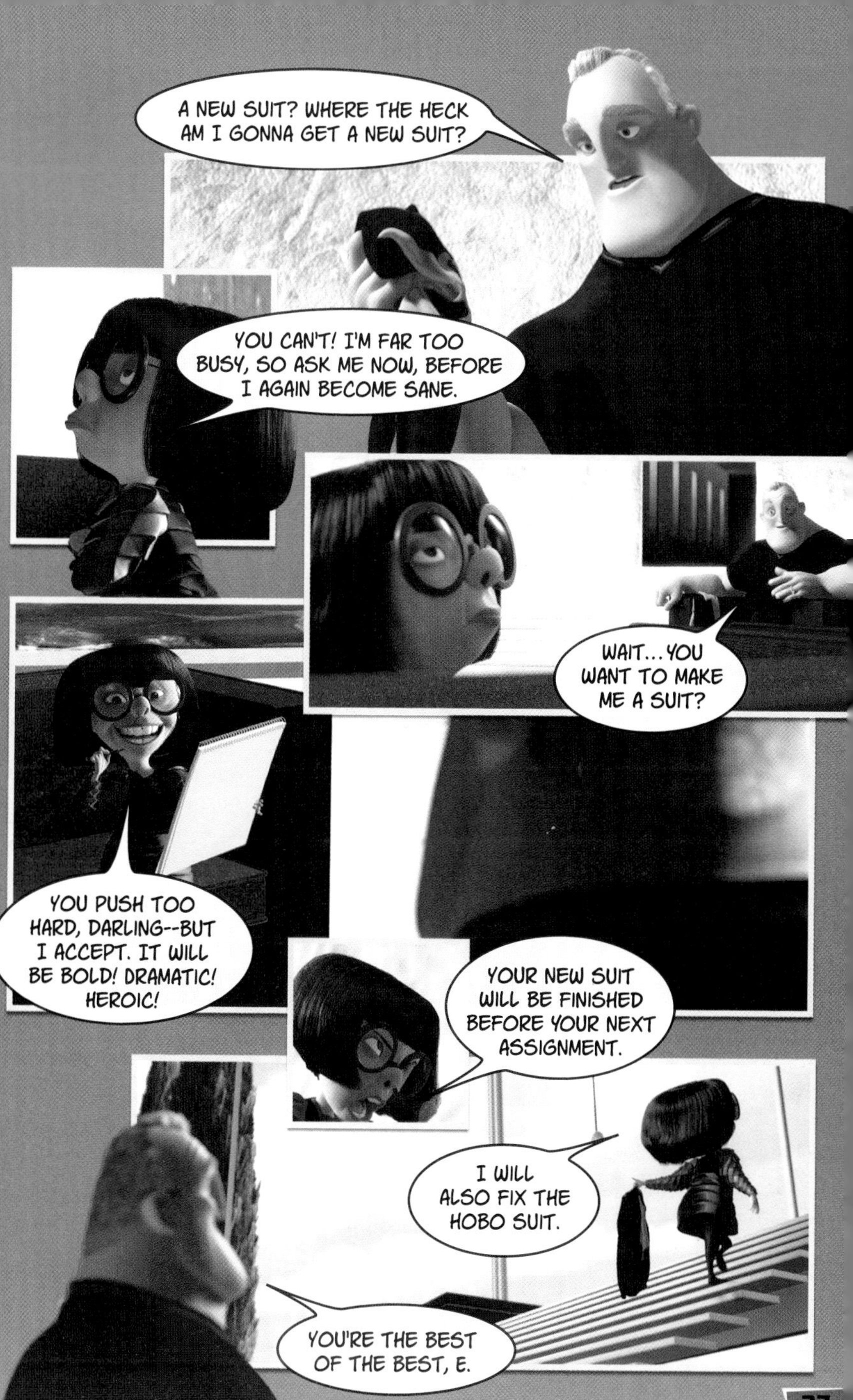
A NEW SUIT? WHERE THE HECK AM I GONNA GET A NEW SUIT?
YOU CAN'T! I'M FAR TOO BUSY, SO ASK ME NOW, BEFORE I AGAIN BECOME SANE.
WAIT... YOU WANT TO MAKE ME A SUIT?
YOU PUSH TOO HARD, DARLING--BUT I ACCEPT. IT WILL BE BOLD! DRAMATIC! HEROIC!
YOUR NEW SUIT WILL BE FINISHED BEFORE YOUR NEXT ASSIGNMENT.
I WILL ALSO FIX THE HOBO SUIT.
YOU'RE THE BEST OF THE BEST, E.

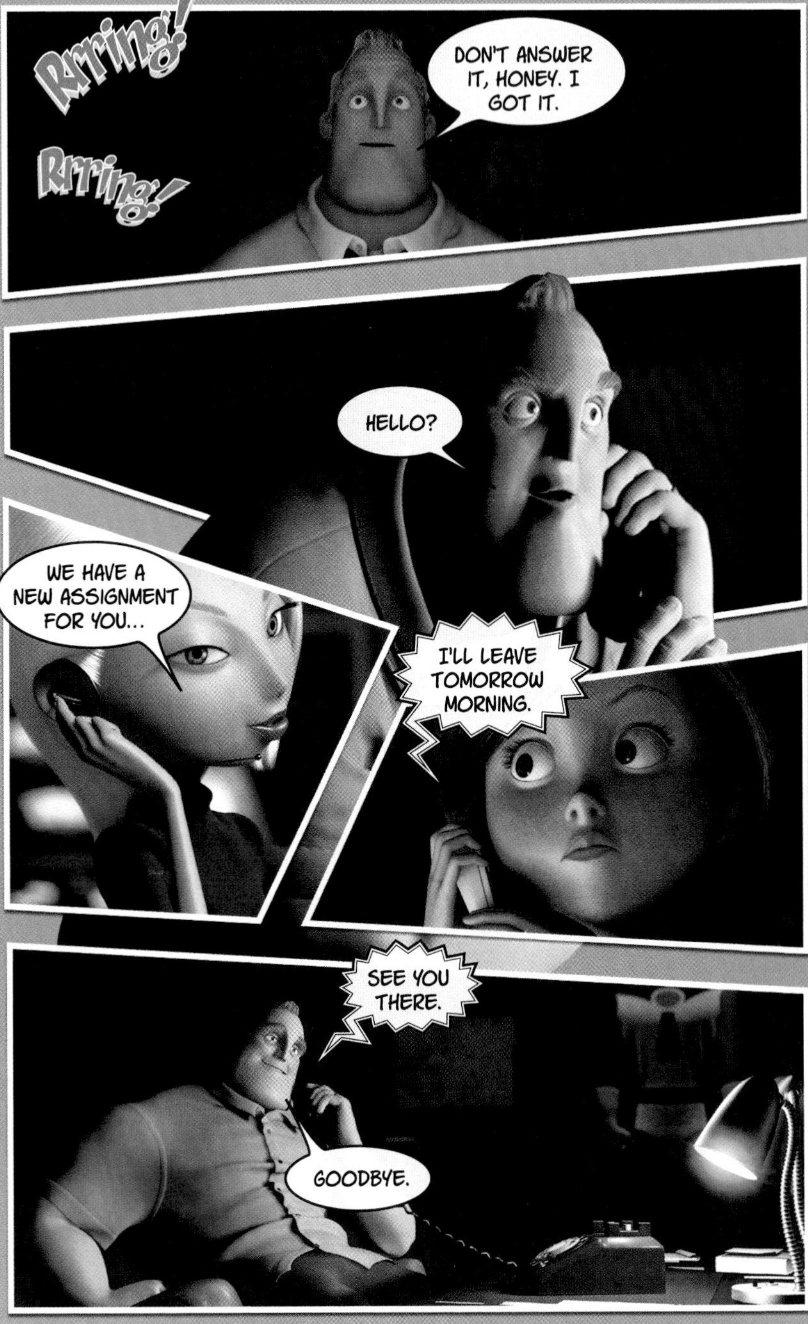
Rrrring!
Rrrring!
DON'T ANSWER IT, HONEY. I GOT IT.
HELLO?
WE HAVE A NEW ASSIGNMENT FOR YOU...
I'LL LEAVE TOMORROW MORNING.
SEE YOU THERE.
GOODBYE.

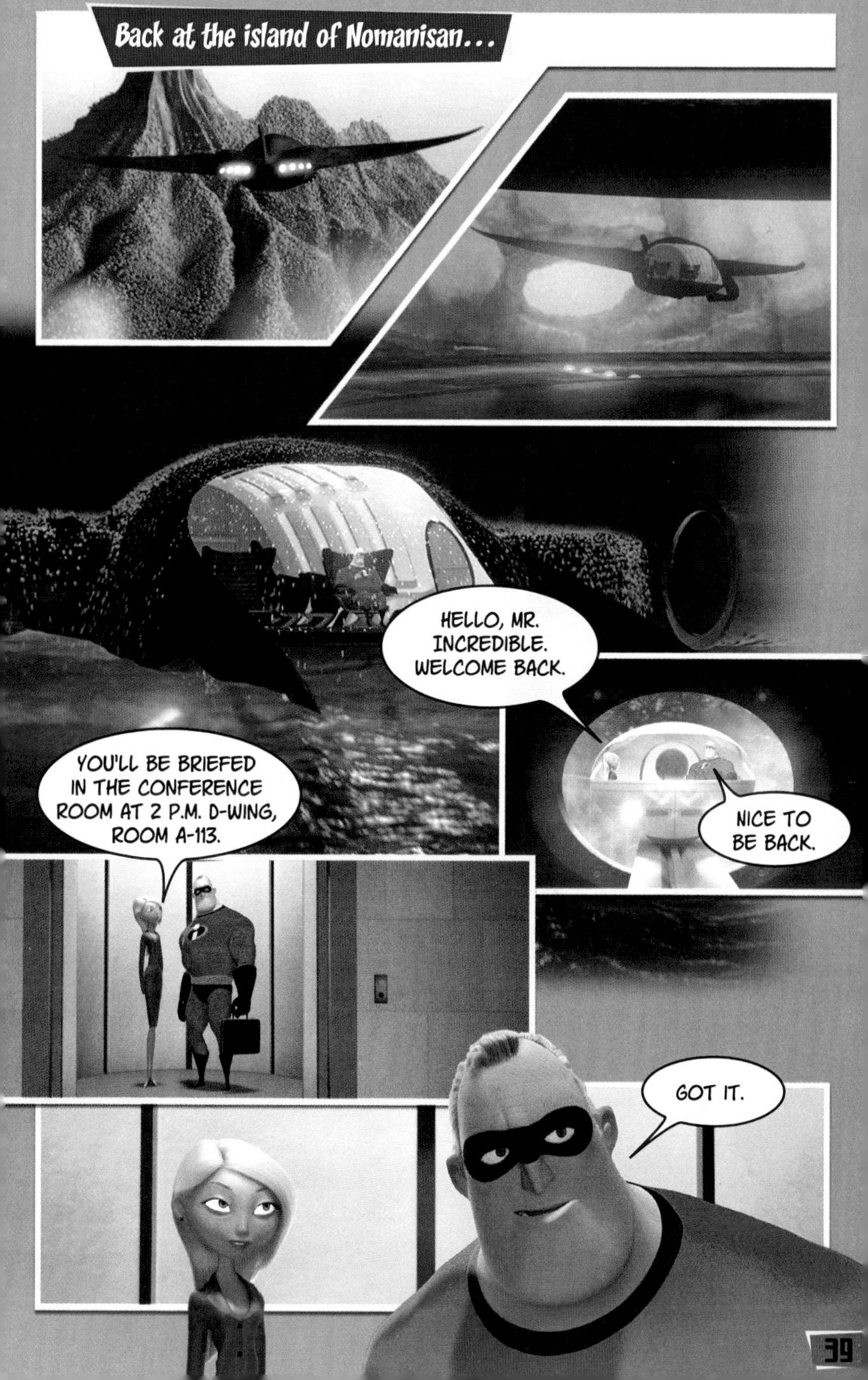
Back at the island of Nomanisan...
HELLO, MR. INCREDIBLE. WELCOME BACK.
NICE TO BE BACK.
YOU'LL BE BRIEFED IN THE CONFERENCE ROOM AT 2 P.M. D-WING, ROOM A-113.
GOT IT.

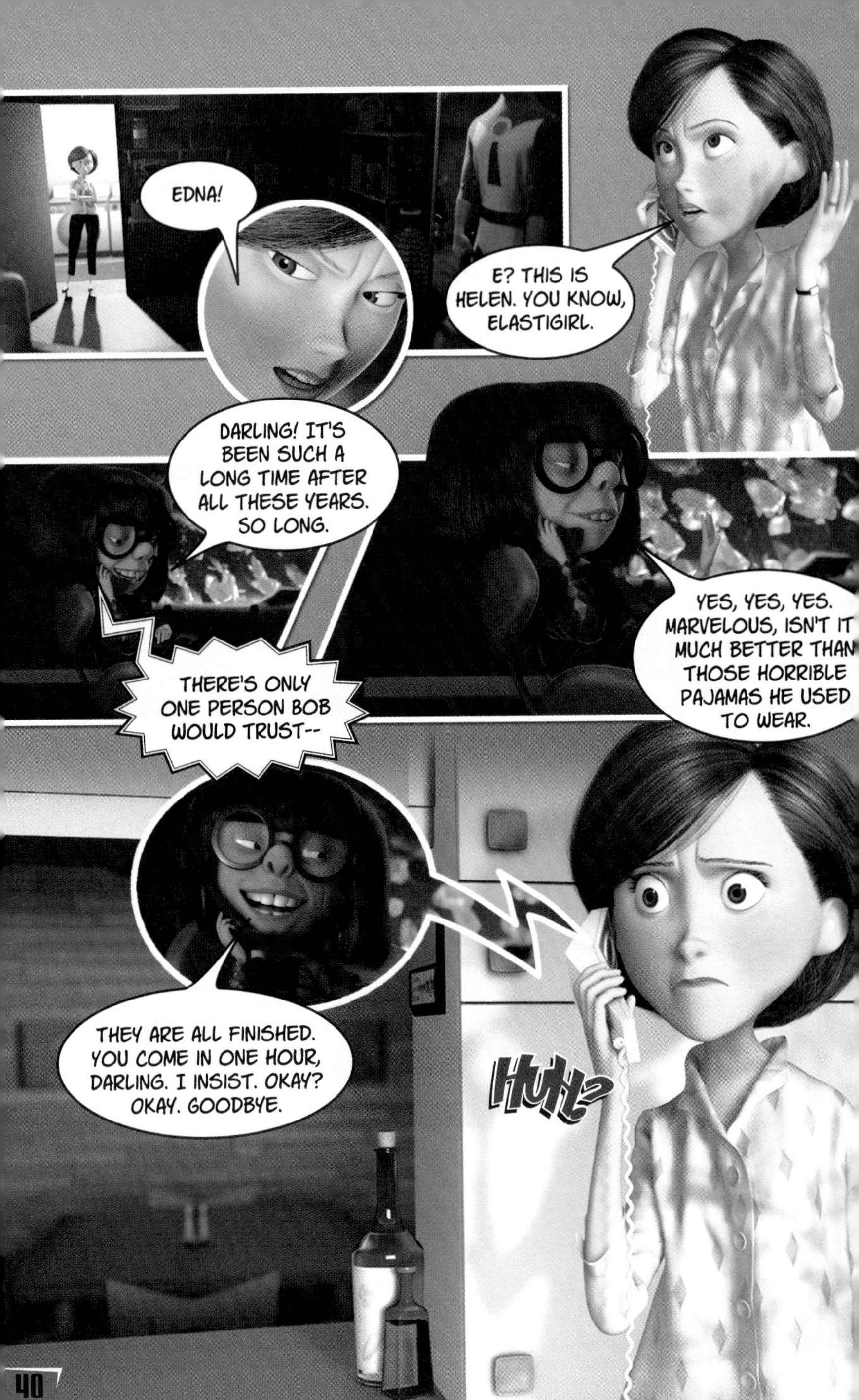
EDNA!
E? THIS IS HELEN. YOU KNOW, ELASTIGIRL.
DARLING! IT'S BEEN SUCH A LONG TIME AFTER ALL THESE YEARS. SO LONG.
THERE'S ONLY ONE PERSON BOB WOULD TRUST--
YES, YES, YES. MARVELOUS, ISN'T IT MUCH BETTER THAN THOSE HORRIBLE PAJAMAS HE USED TO WEAR.
THEY ARE ALL FINISHED. YOU COME IN ONE HOUR, DARLING. I INSIST. OKAY? OKAY. GOODBYE.
HUH?

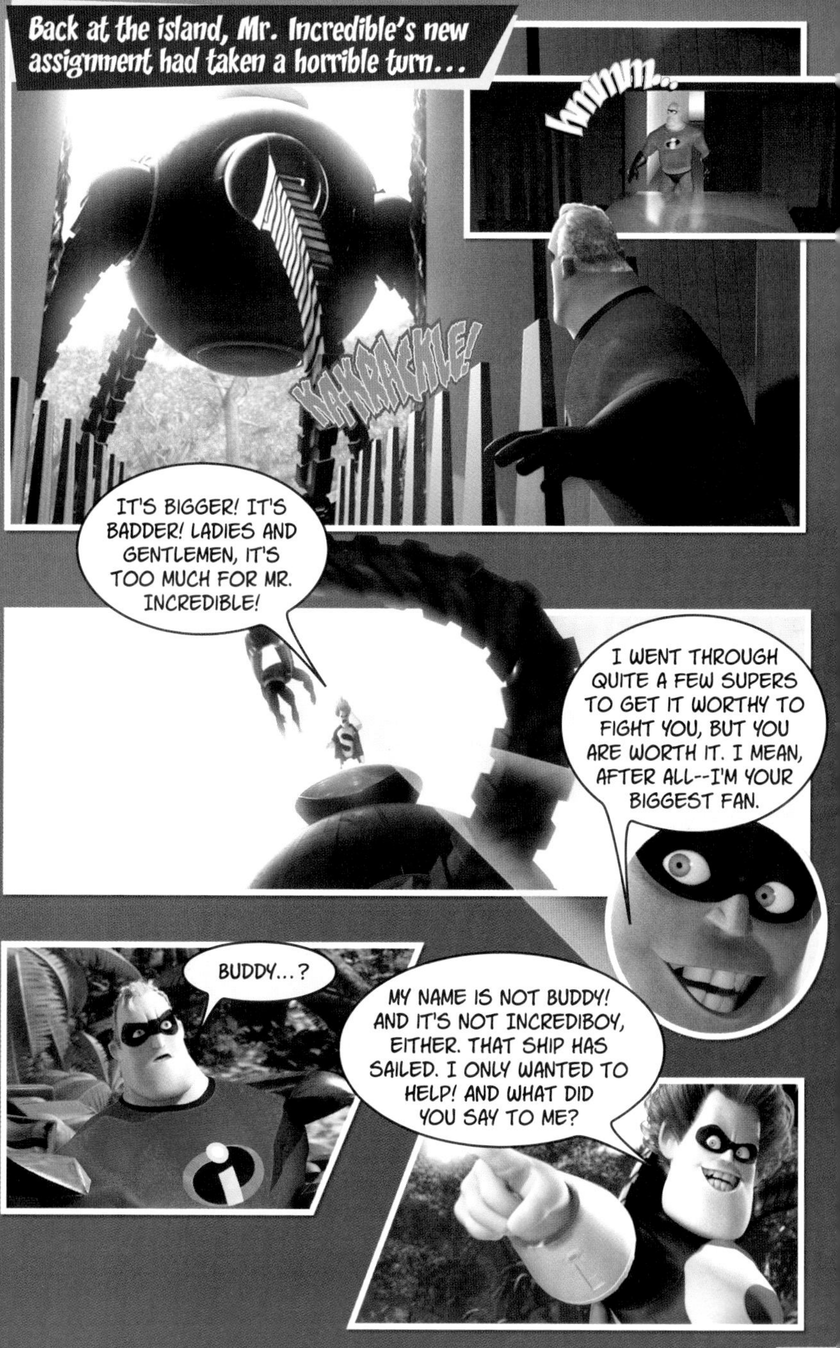
Back at the island, Mr. Incredible's new assignment had taken a horrible turn...
KA-KRACKLE!
IT'S BIGGER! IT'S BADDER! LADIES AND GENTLEMEN, IT'S TOO MUCH FOR MR. INCREDIBLE!
I WENT THROUGH QUITE A FEW SUPERS TO GET IT WORTHY TO FIGHT YOU, BUT YOU ARE WORTH IT. I MEAN, AFTER ALL--I'M YOUR BIGGEST FAN.
BUDDY...?
MY NAME IS NOT BUDDY! AND IT'S NOT INCREDIBOY, EITHER. THAT SHIP HAS SAILED. I ONLY WANTED TO HELP! AND WHAT DID YOU SAY TO ME?

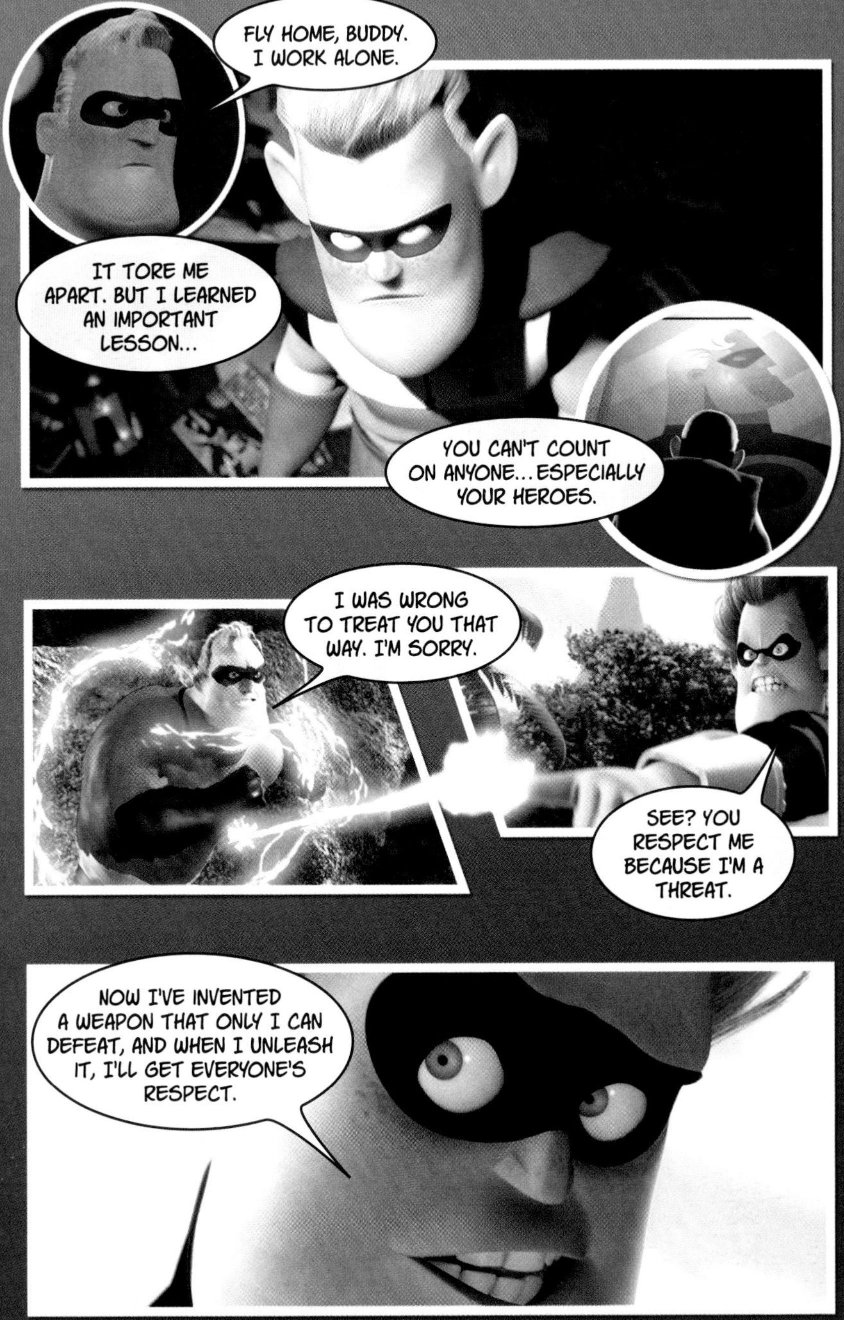
FLY HOME, BUDDY. I WORK ALONE.
IT TORE ME APART. BUT I LEARNED AN IMPORTANT LESSON...
YOU CAN'T COUNT ON ANYONE... ESPECIALLY YOUR HEROES.
I WAS WRONG TO TREAT YOU THAT WAY. I'M SORRY.
SEE? YOU RESPECT ME BECAUSE I'M A THREAT.
NOW I'VE INVENTED A WEAPON THAT ONLY I CAN DEFEAT, AND WHEN I UNLEASH IT, I'LL GET EVERYONE'S RESPECT.

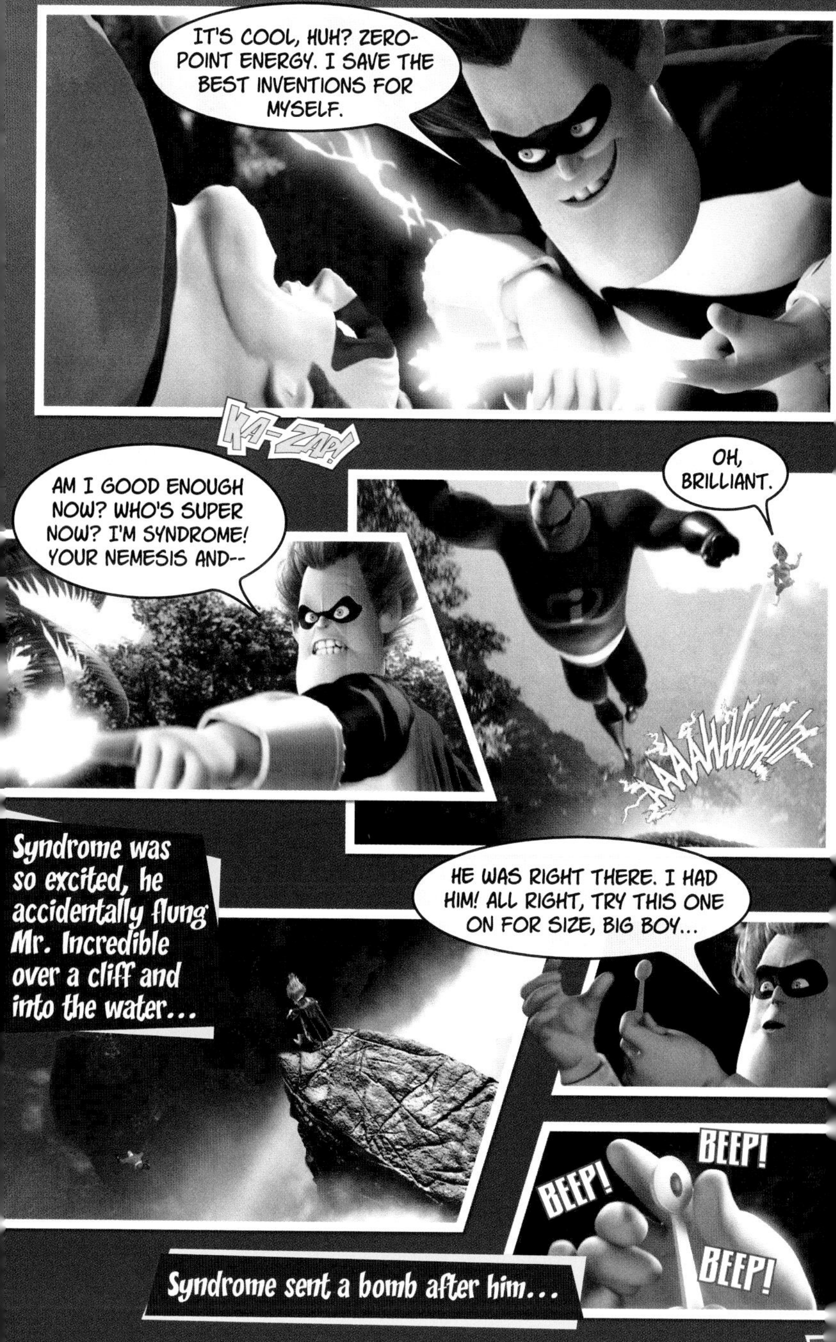
IT'S COOL, HUH? ZERO-POINT ENERGY. I SAVE THE BEST INVENTIONS FOR MYSELF.
KA-ZAP!
AM I GOOD ENOUGH NOW? WHO'S SUPER NOW? I'M SYNDROME! YOUR NEMESIS AND--
OH, BRILLIANT.
AAAAHHHH!!!
Syndrome was so excited, he accidentally flung Mr. Incredible over a cliff and into the water...
HE WAS RIGHT THERE. I HAD HIM! ALL RIGHT, TRY THIS ONE ON FOR SIZE, BIG BOY...
BEEP!
BEEP!
BEEP!
Syndrome sent a bomb after him...

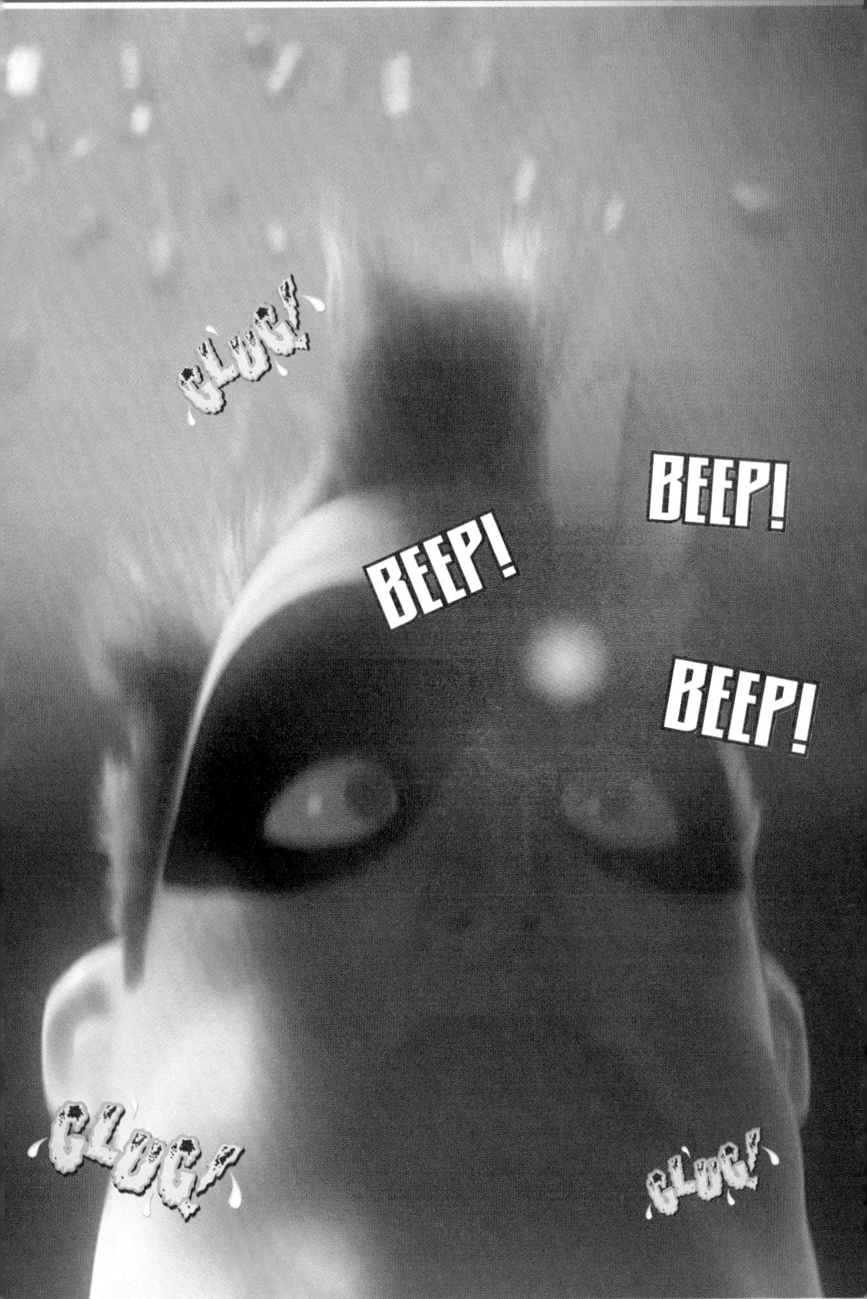
CLUG!
BEEP!
BEEP!
BEEP!
CLUG!
CLUG!

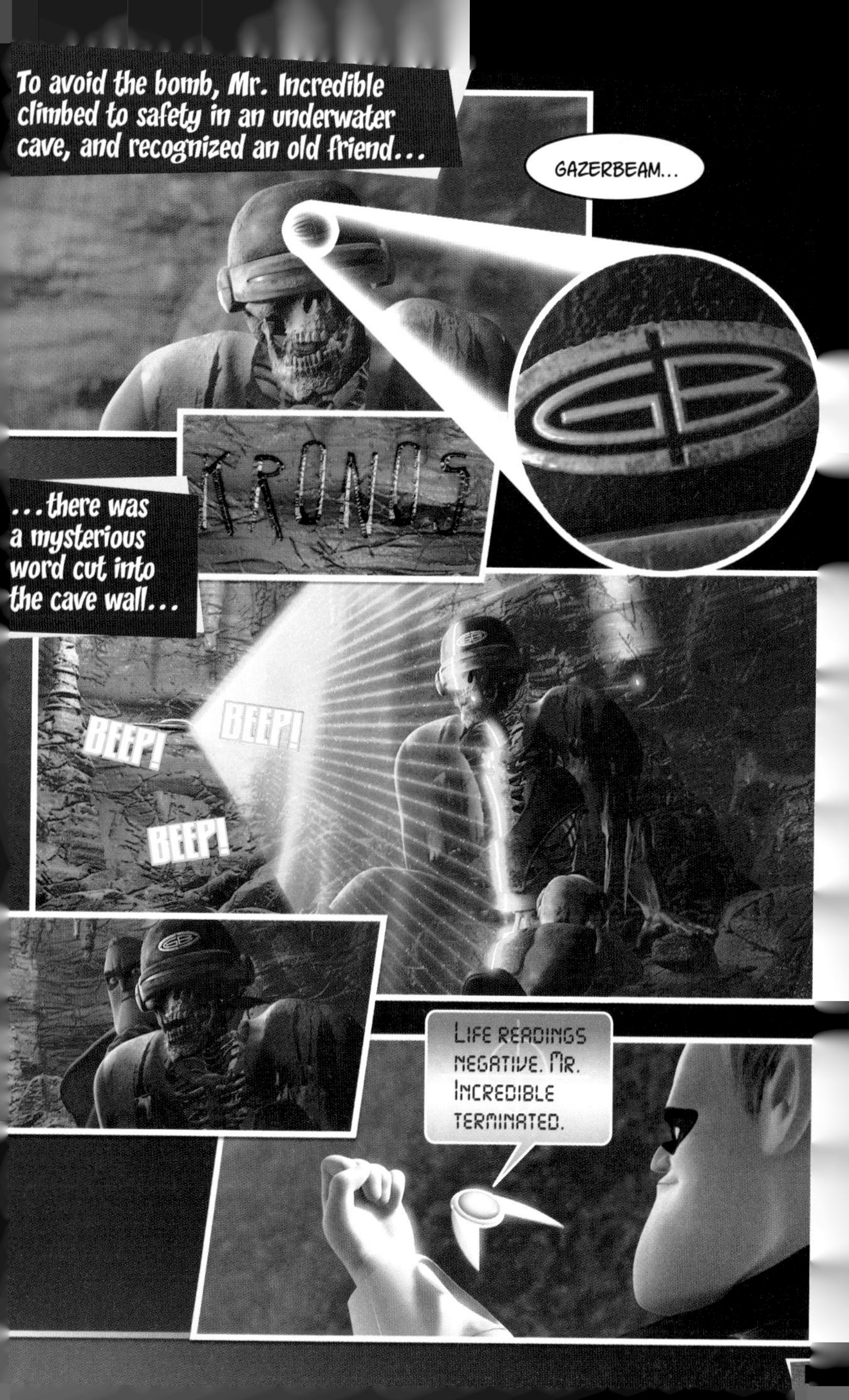
To avoid the bomb, Mr. Incredible climbed to safety in an underwater cave, and recognized an old friend...
GAZERBEAM...
KRONOS
...there was a mysterious word cut into the cave wall...
BEEP!
BEEP!
BEEP!
LIFE READINGS NEGATIVE. MR. INCREDIBLE TERMINATED.

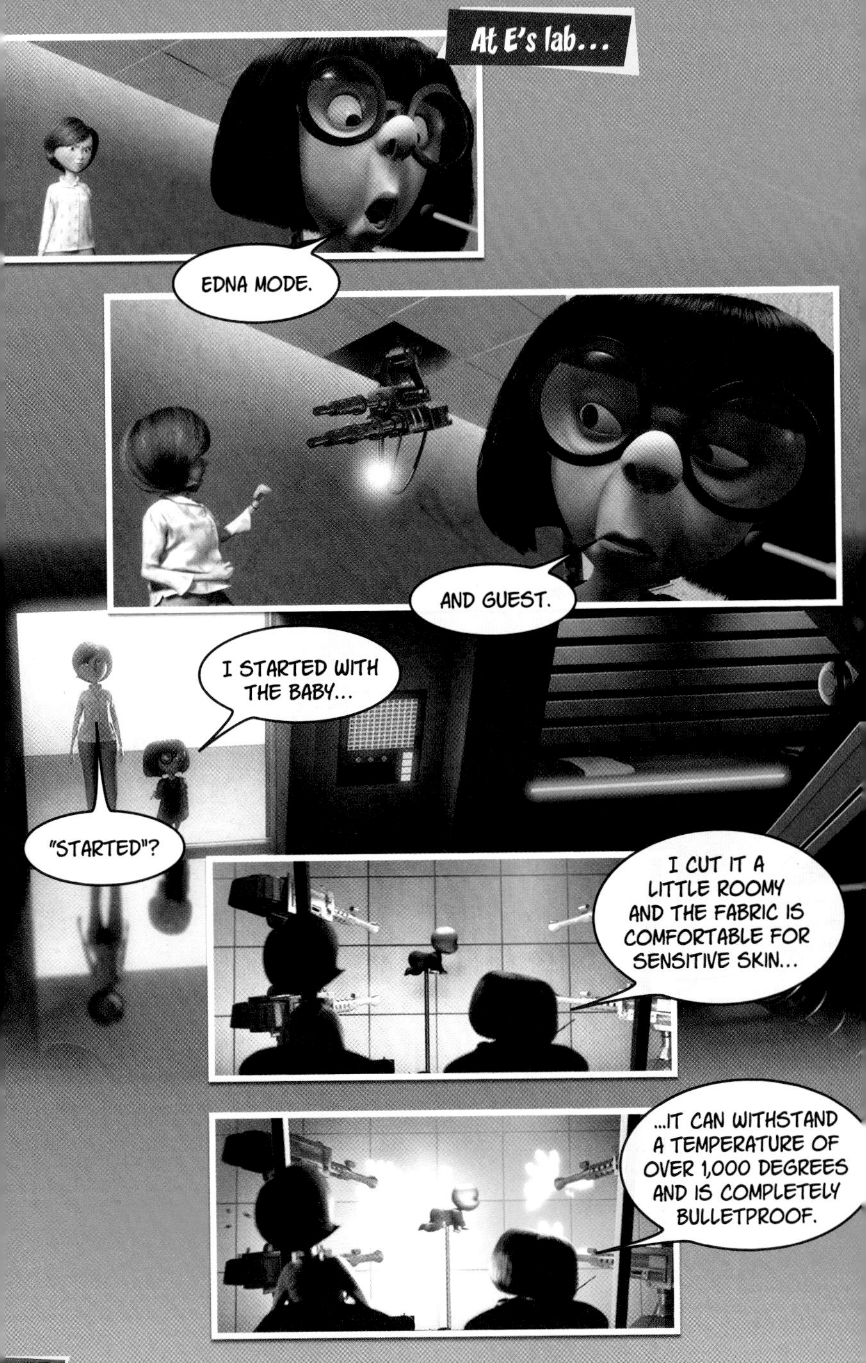
At E's lab...
EDNA MODE.
AND GUEST.
I STARTED WITH THE BABY...
"STARTED"?
I CUT IT A LITTLE ROOMY AND THE FABRIC IS COMFORTABLE FOR SENSITIVE SKIN...
...IT CAN WITHSTAND A TEMPERATURE OF OVER 1,000 DEGREES AND IS COMPLETELY BULLETPROOF.

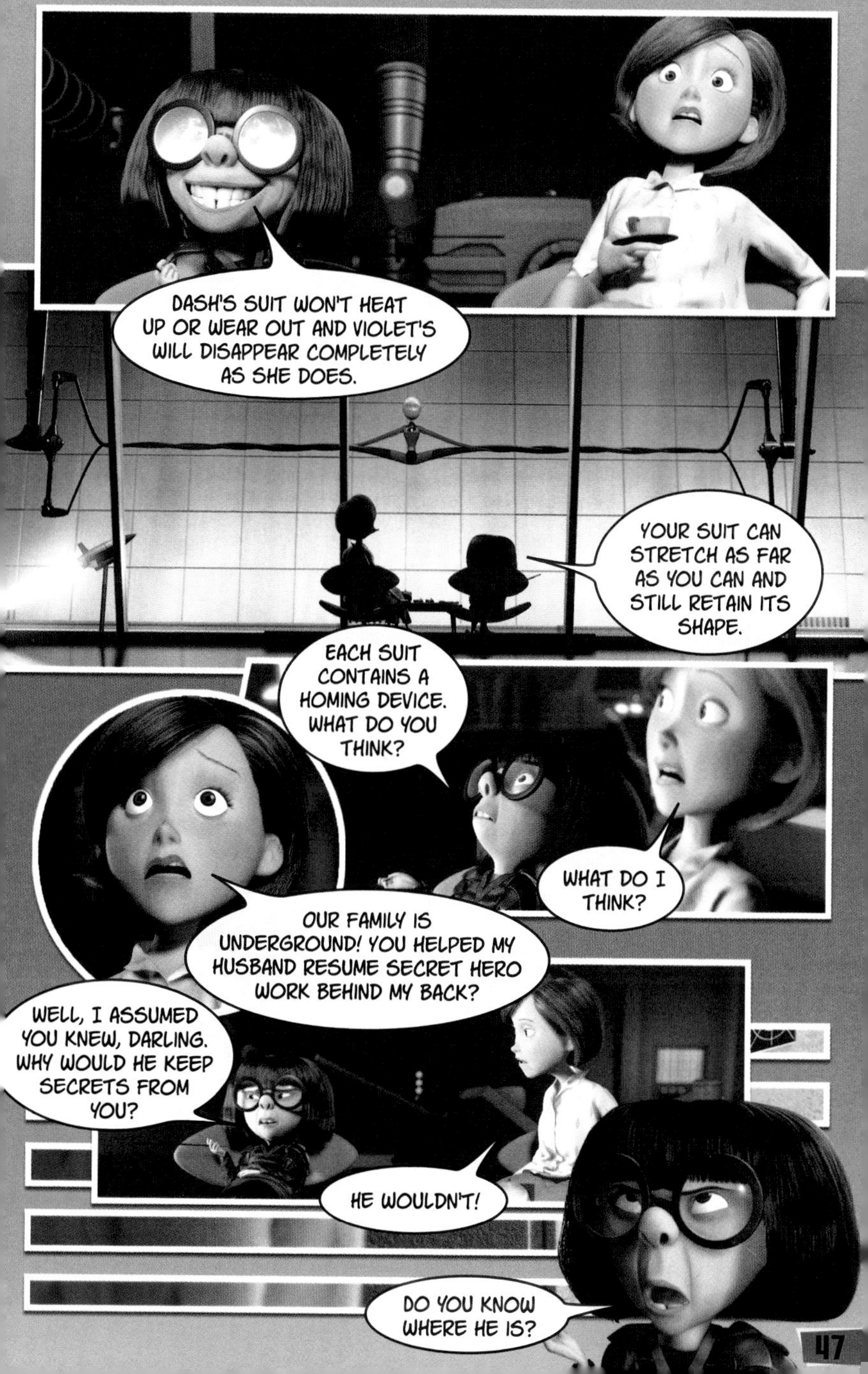
DASH'S SUIT WON'T HEAT UP OR WEAR OUT AND VIOLET'S WILL DISAPPEAR COMPLETELY AS SHE DOES.
YOUR SUIT CAN STRETCH AS FAR AS YOU CAN AND STILL RETAIN ITS SHAPE.
EACH SUIT CONTAINS A HOMING DEVICE. WHAT DO YOU THINK?
WHAT DO I THINK?
OUR FAMILY IS UNDERGROUND! YOU HELPED MY HUSBAND RESUME SECRET HERO WORK BEHIND MY BACK?
WELL, I ASSUMED YOU KNEW, DARLING. WHY WOULD HE KEEP SECRETS FROM YOU?
HE WOULDN'T!
DO YOU KNOW WHERE HE IS?

After sneaking back onto the base, Mr. Incredible used Gazerbeam's clue to break into Syndrome's computer system.

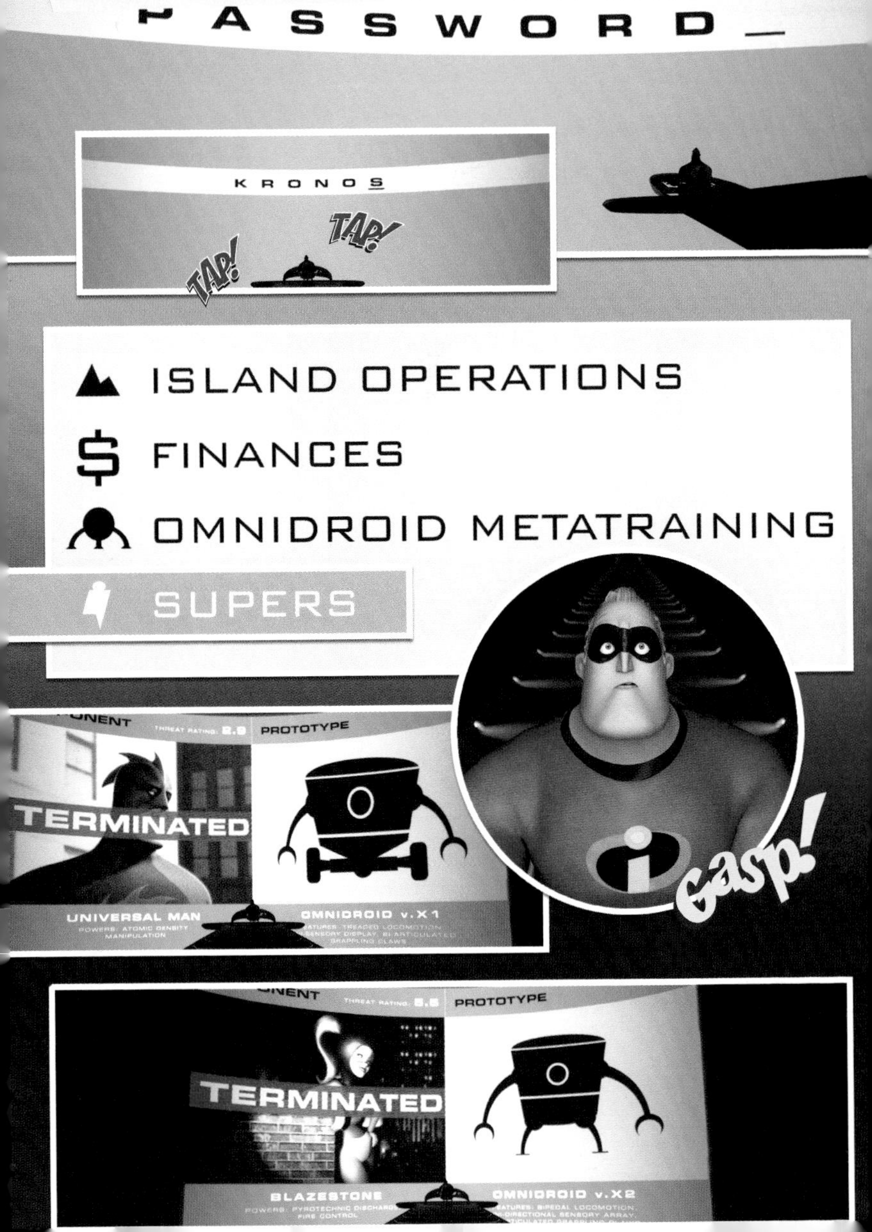
ASSWORD_
KRONOS
TAP!
TAP!
ISLAND OPERATIONS
FINANCES
OMNIDROID METATRAINING
SUPERS
PROTOTYPE
TERMINATED
UNIVERSAL MAN
POWERS: ATOMIC DENSITY MANIPULATION
OMNIDROID v.X1
Gasp!
PROTOTYPE
TERMINATED
BLAZESTONE
POWERS: PYROTECHNIC DISCHARGE FIRE CONTROL
OMNIDROID v.X2

OPPONENT · THREAT RATING: 8.8 · PROTOTYPE

TERMINATED

DOWNBURST
POWERS: FLIGHT
HAZARDOUS EXPULSION

OMNIDROID v.X3
SUSPENDED TRI-PEDAL LOCOMOTION
SLASHING CLAWS, UNI-DIRECTIONAL
SENSORY ARRAY

OPPONENT · THREAT RATING: 8.8 · PROTOTYPE

TERMINATED

APOGEE
POWERS: GRAVITY CONTROL
LEVITATION

OMNIDROID v.X4
POWERS: QUADRA-PEDAL LOCOMOTION
SLASHING CLAWS, QUADRA-DIRECTIONAL
SENSORY ARRAY

ELASTIGIRL

FULL-BODY ELASTICITY, BODY CAPABLE OF STRETCHING IN
STRETCHING
EXP
LAST ACTIVE RECORD 13.11.55

LOCATION: UNKNOWN

THREAT RATING: 8.2 EXERCISE MODERATE CAUTION

SEARCH | MR. INCREDIBLE

OPPONENT · THREAT RATING: 8.1 · PROTOTYPE

TERMINATED

MR. INCREDIBLE
SUPER-HUMAN STRENGTH CAPABLE OF LIFTING 100,000 LBS
INVULNERABILITY TO HIGH LEVELS OF PHYSICAL

OPERATION KRONOS

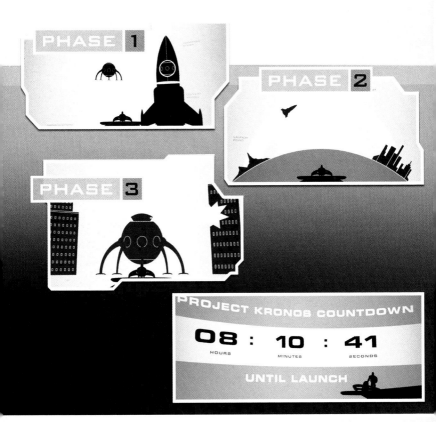

PHASE 1

PHASE 2

PHASE 3

PROJECT KRONOS COUNTDOWN

08 : 10 : 41

HOURS   MINUTES   SECONDS

UNTIL LAUNCH

10 : 40

MINUTES   OH NO!   SECONDS

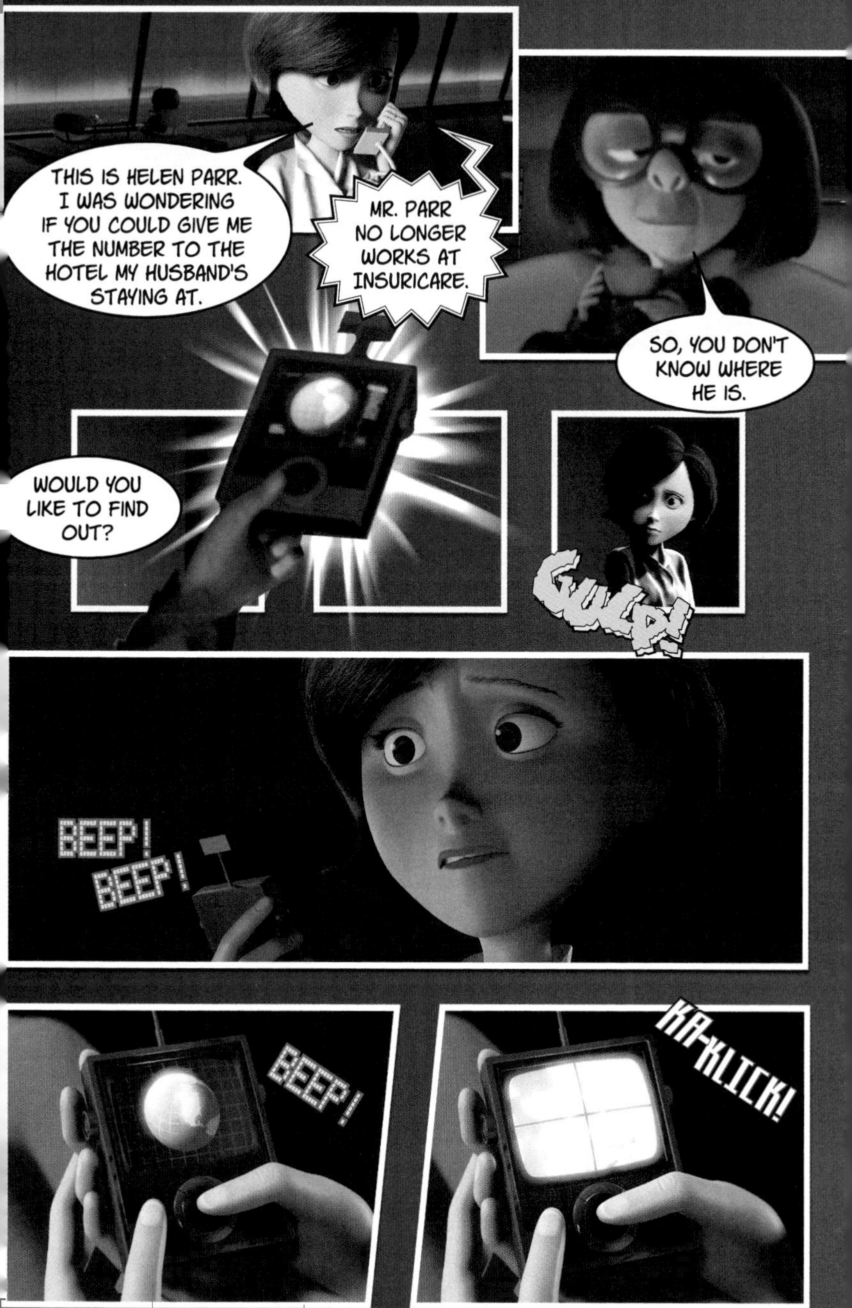
THIS IS HELEN PARR. I WAS WONDERING IF YOU COULD GIVE ME THE NUMBER TO THE HOTEL MY HUSBAND'S STAYING AT.
MR. PARR NO LONGER WORKS AT INSURICARE.
SO, YOU DON'T KNOW WHERE HE IS.
WOULD YOU LIKE TO FIND OUT?
GULP!
BEEP! BEEP!
BEEP!
KA-KLICK!

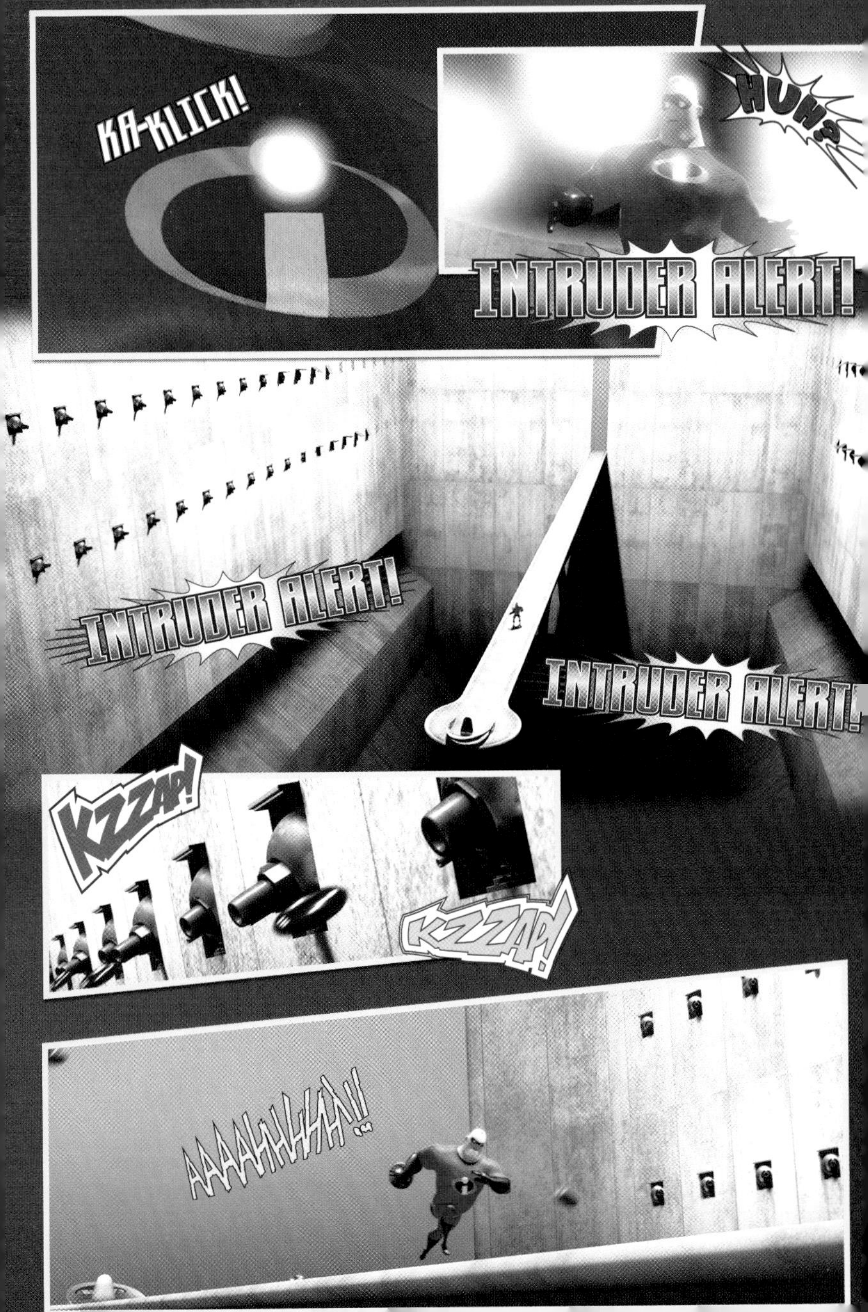
KA-KLICK!
HUH?
INTRUDER ALERT!
INTRUDER ALERT!
INTRUDER ALERT!
KZZAP!
KZZAP!
AAAAHHHHHH!!

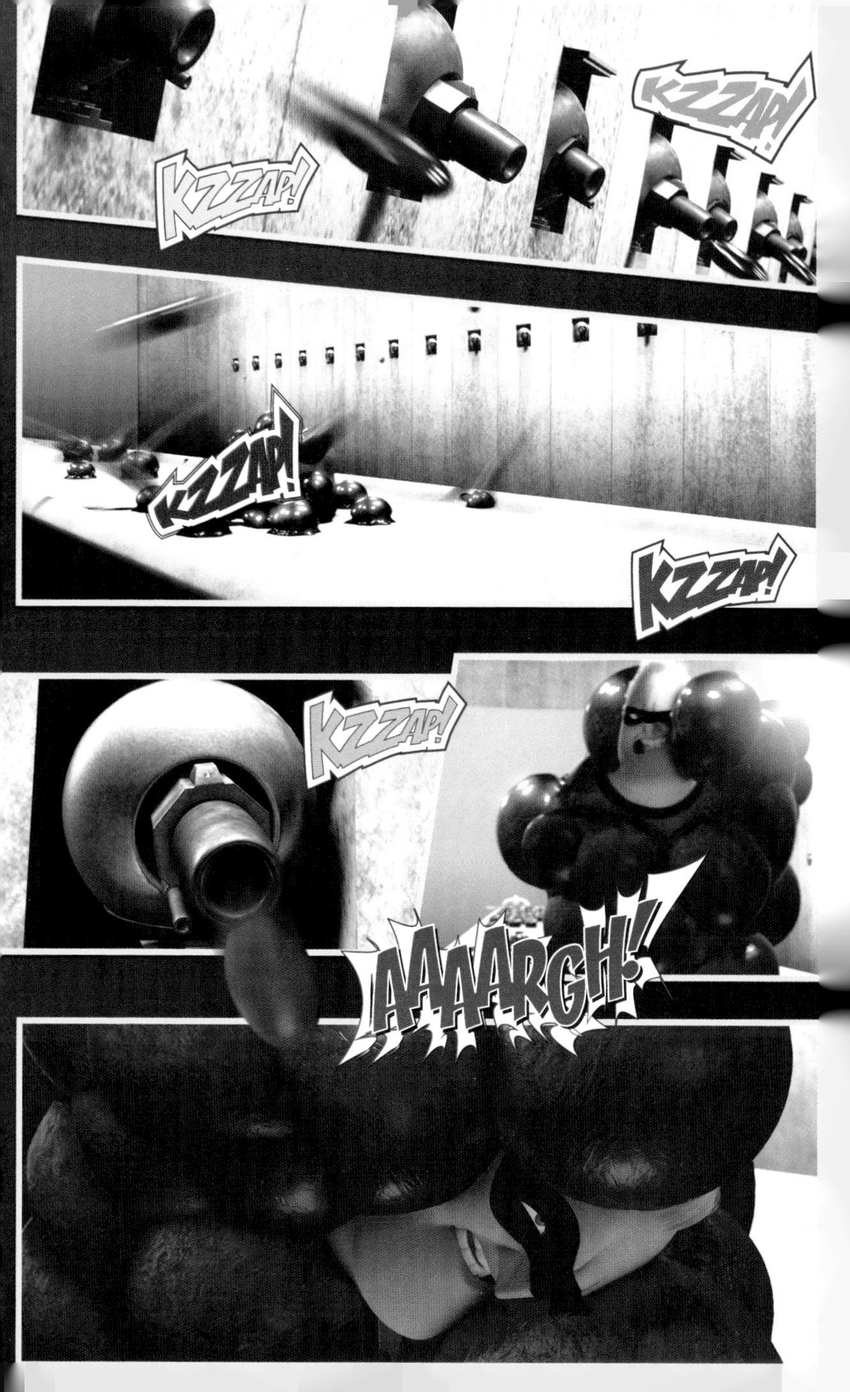
KZZAP!
KZZAP!
KZZAP!
KZZAP!
KZZAP!
AAAARGH!

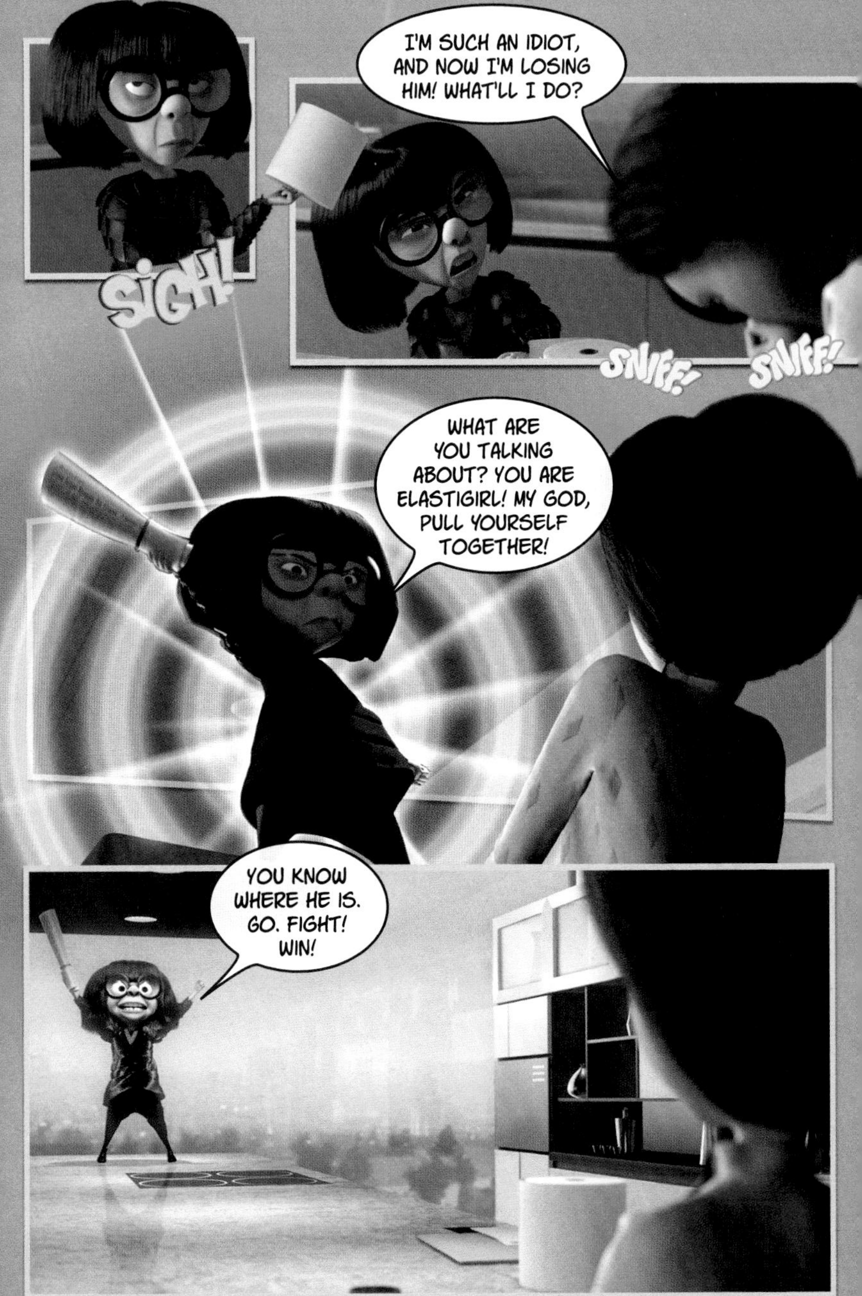
SIGH!
I'M SUCH AN IDIOT, AND NOW I'M LOSING HIM! WHAT'LL I DO?
SNIFF!
SNIFF!
WHAT ARE YOU TALKING ABOUT? YOU ARE ELASTIGIRL! MY GOD, PULL YOURSELF TOGETHER!
YOU KNOW WHERE HE IS. GO. FIGHT! WIN!

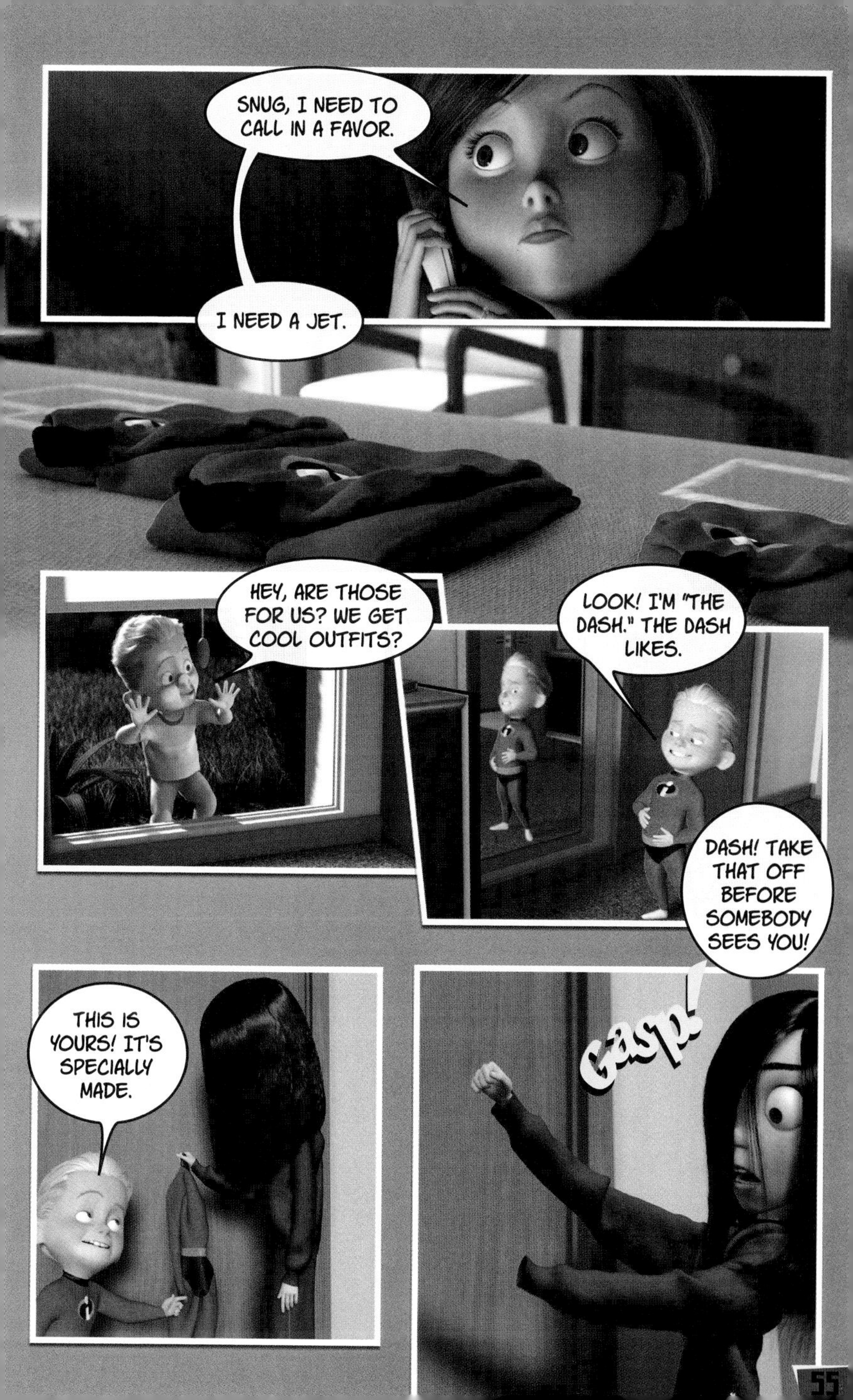
SNUG, I NEED TO CALL IN A FAVOR.
I NEED A JET.
HEY, ARE THOSE FOR US? WE GET COOL OUTFITS?
LOOK! I'M "THE DASH." THE DASH LIKES.
DASH! TAKE THAT OFF BEFORE SOMEBODY SEES YOU!
THIS IS YOURS! IT'S SPECIALLY MADE.
Gasp!

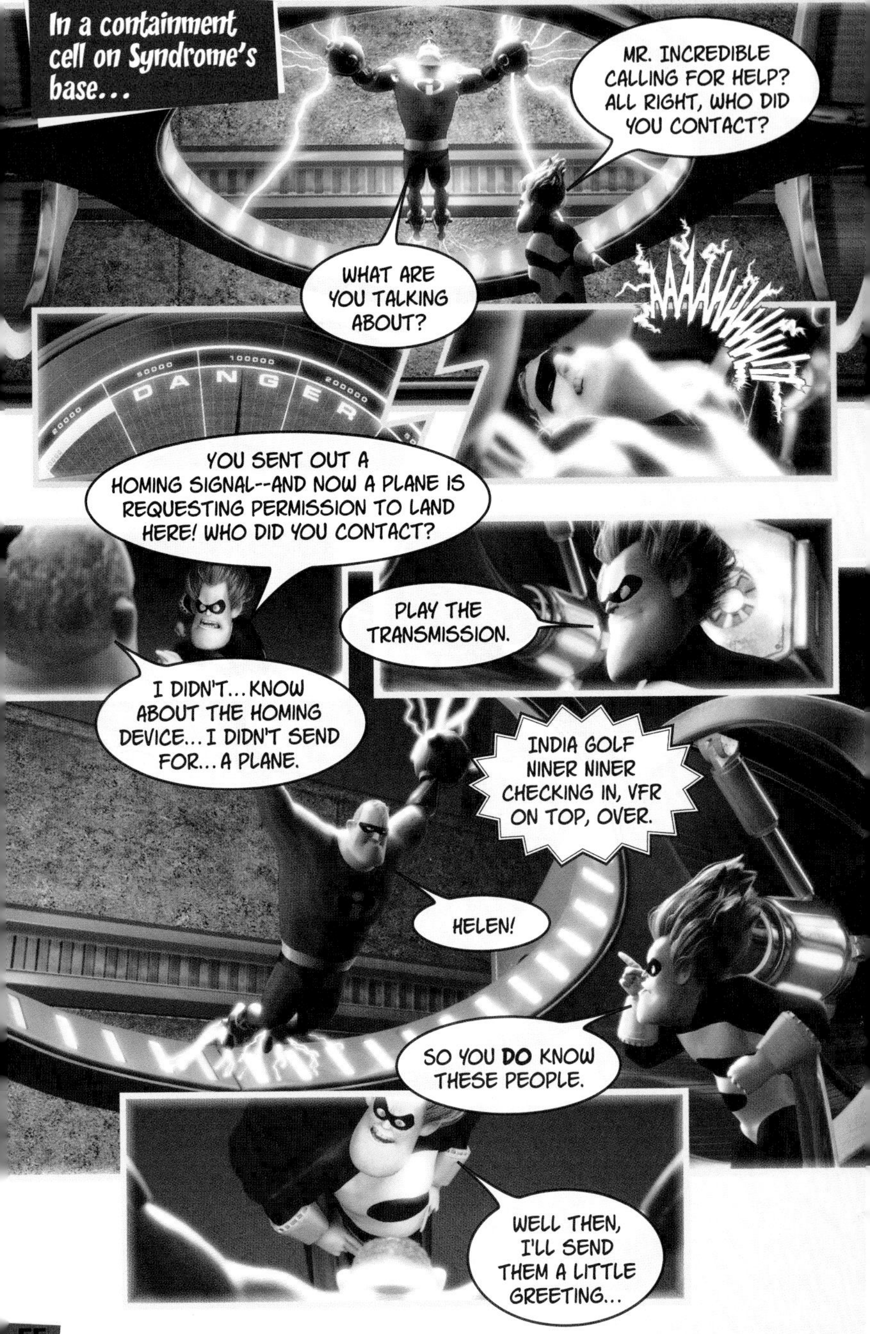
In a containment cell on Syndrome's base...
MR. INCREDIBLE CALLING FOR HELP? ALL RIGHT, WHO DID YOU CONTACT?
WHAT ARE YOU TALKING ABOUT?
AAAAHHHH!!!
YOU SENT OUT A HOMING SIGNAL--AND NOW A PLANE IS REQUESTING PERMISSION TO LAND HERE! WHO DID YOU CONTACT?
I DIDN'T... KNOW ABOUT THE HOMING DEVICE... I DIDN'T SEND FOR... A PLANE.
PLAY THE TRANSMISSION.
INDIA GOLF NINER NINER CHECKING IN, VFR ON TOP, OVER.
HELEN!
SO YOU **DO** KNOW THESE PEOPLE.
WELL THEN, I'LL SEND THEM A LITTLE GREETING...

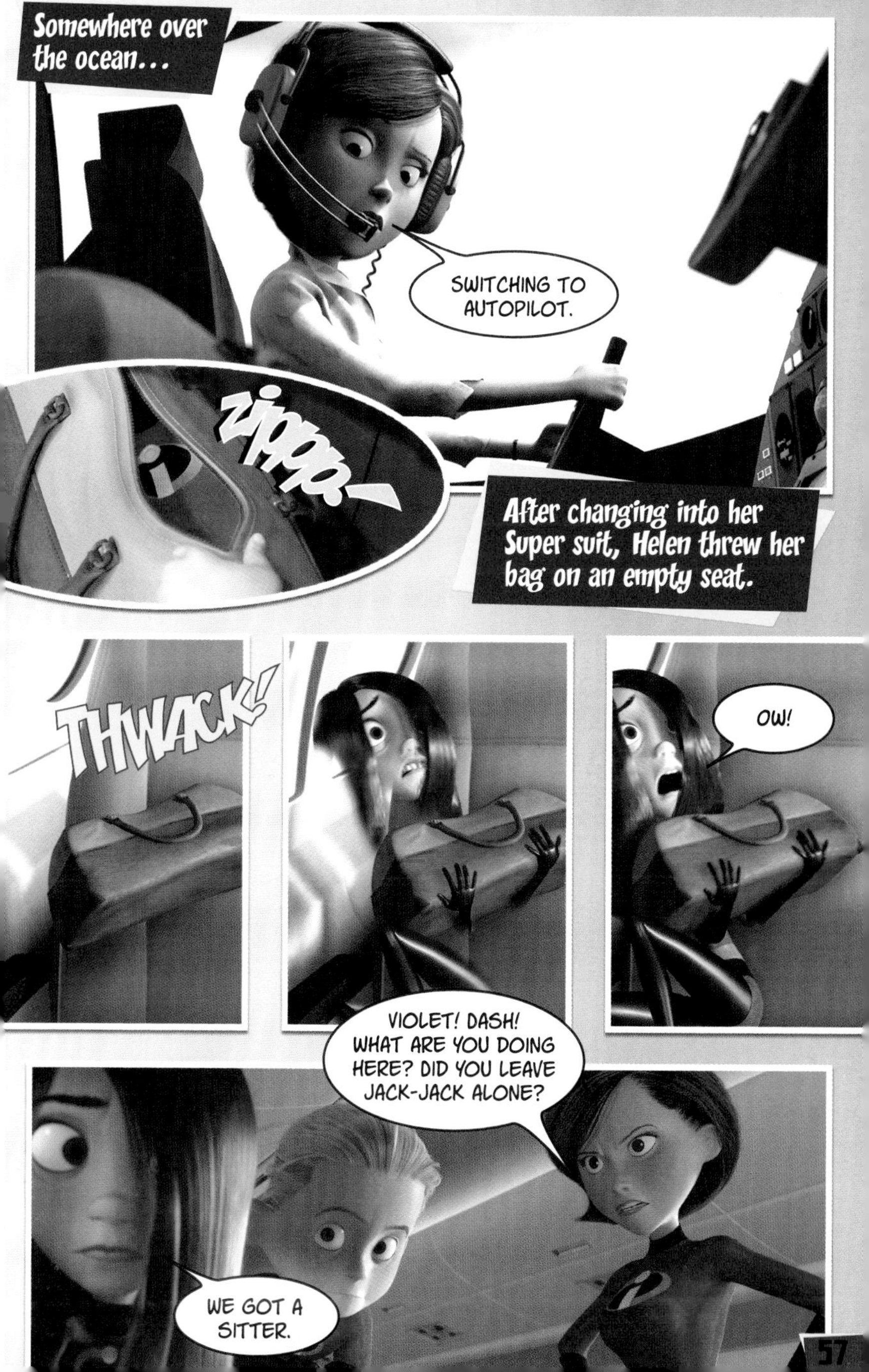
Somewhere over the ocean...
SWITCHING TO AUTOPILOT.
zippp!
After changing into her Super suit, Helen threw her bag on an empty seat.
THWACK!
OW!
VIOLET! DASH! WHAT ARE YOU DOING HERE? DID YOU LEAVE JACK-JACK ALONE?
WE GOT A SITTER.

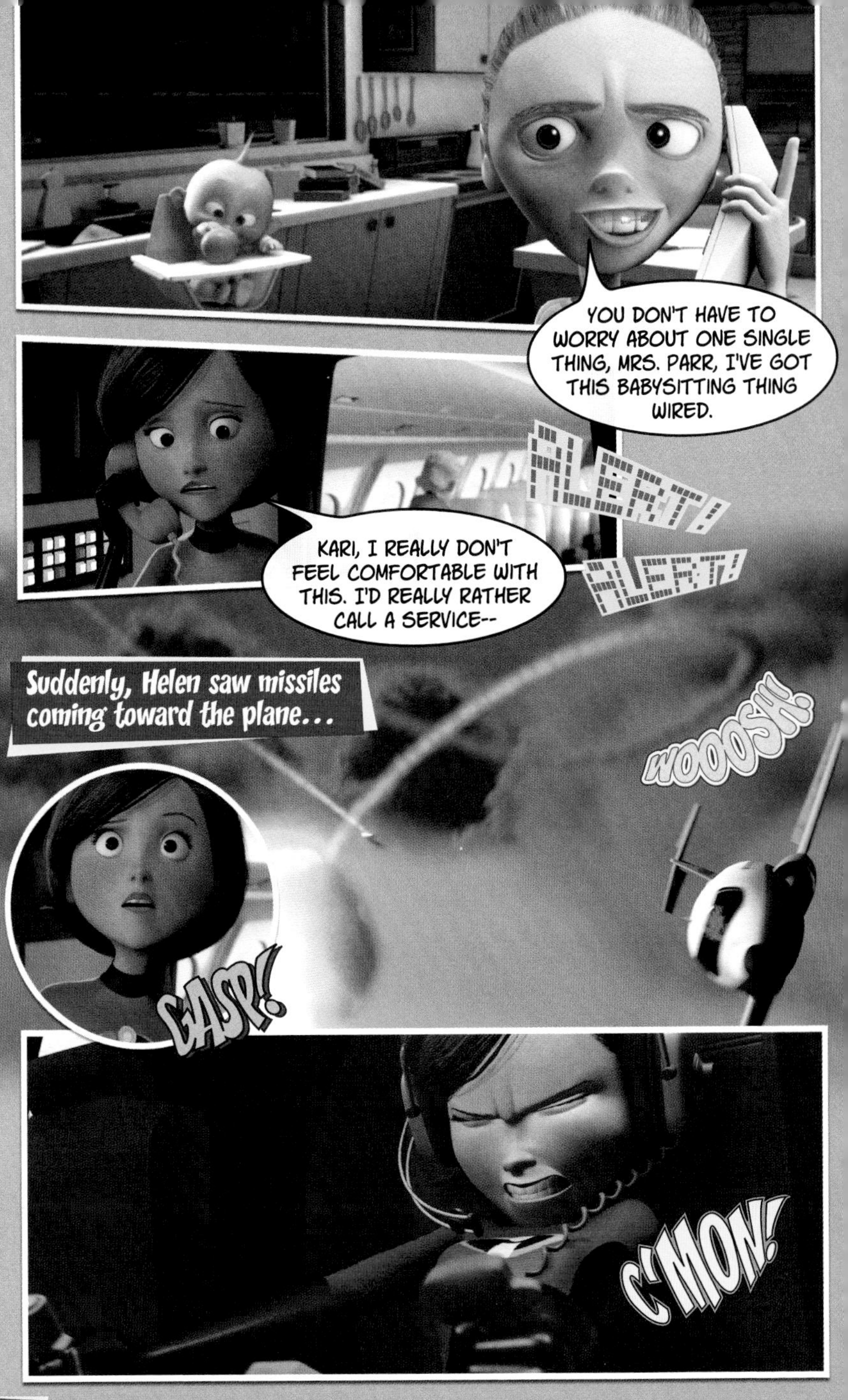
YOU DON'T HAVE TO WORRY ABOUT ONE SINGLE THING, MRS. PARR, I'VE GOT THIS BABYSITTING THING WIRED.
KARI, I REALLY DON'T FEEL COMFORTABLE WITH THIS. I'D REALLY RATHER CALL A SERVICE--
ALERT!
ALERT!
Suddenly, Helen saw missiles coming toward the plane...
WOOOSH!
GASP!
C'MON!

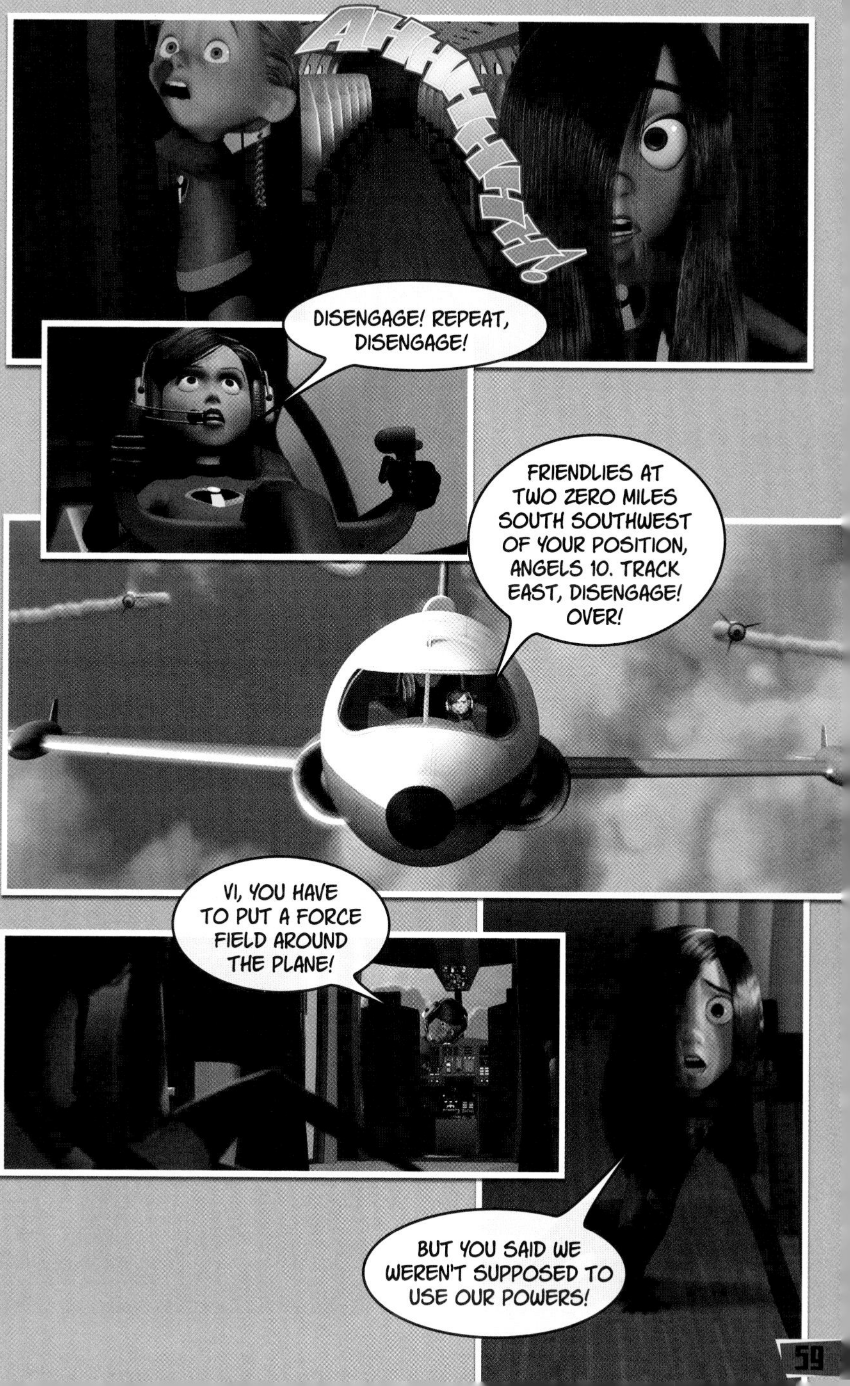

AHHHHHH!
DISENGAGE! REPEAT, DISENGAGE!
FRIENDLIES AT TWO ZERO MILES SOUTH SOUTHWEST OF YOUR POSITION, ANGELS 10. TRACK EAST, DISENGAGE! OVER!
VI, YOU HAVE TO PUT A FORCE FIELD AROUND THE PLANE!
BUT YOU SAID WE WEREN'T SUPPOSED TO USE OUR POWERS!

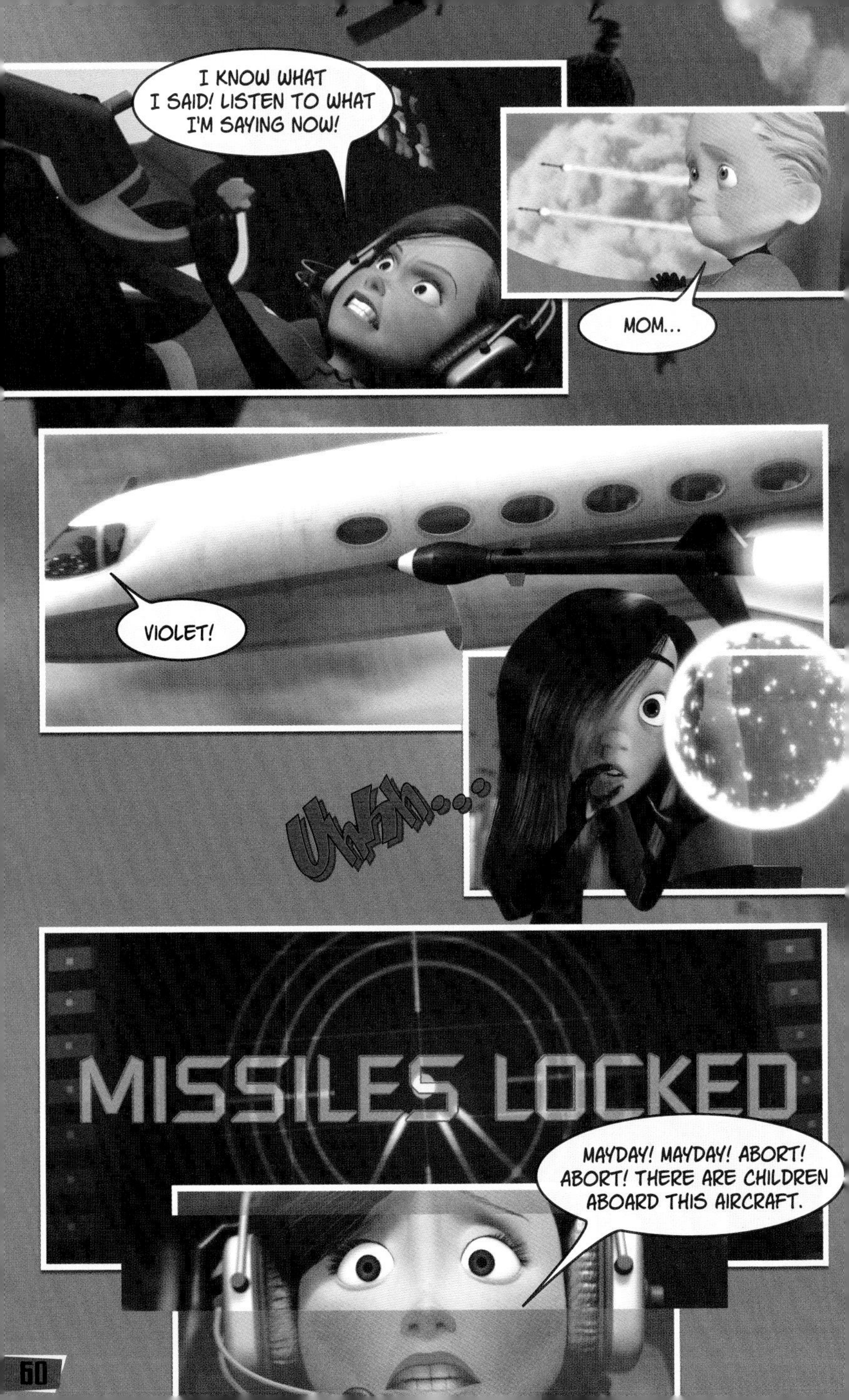
I KNOW WHAT I SAID! LISTEN TO WHAT I'M SAYING NOW!
MOM...
VIOLET!
UHHH...
MISSILES LOCKED
MAYDAY! MAYDAY! ABORT! ABORT! THERE ARE CHILDREN ABOARD THIS AIRCRAFT.

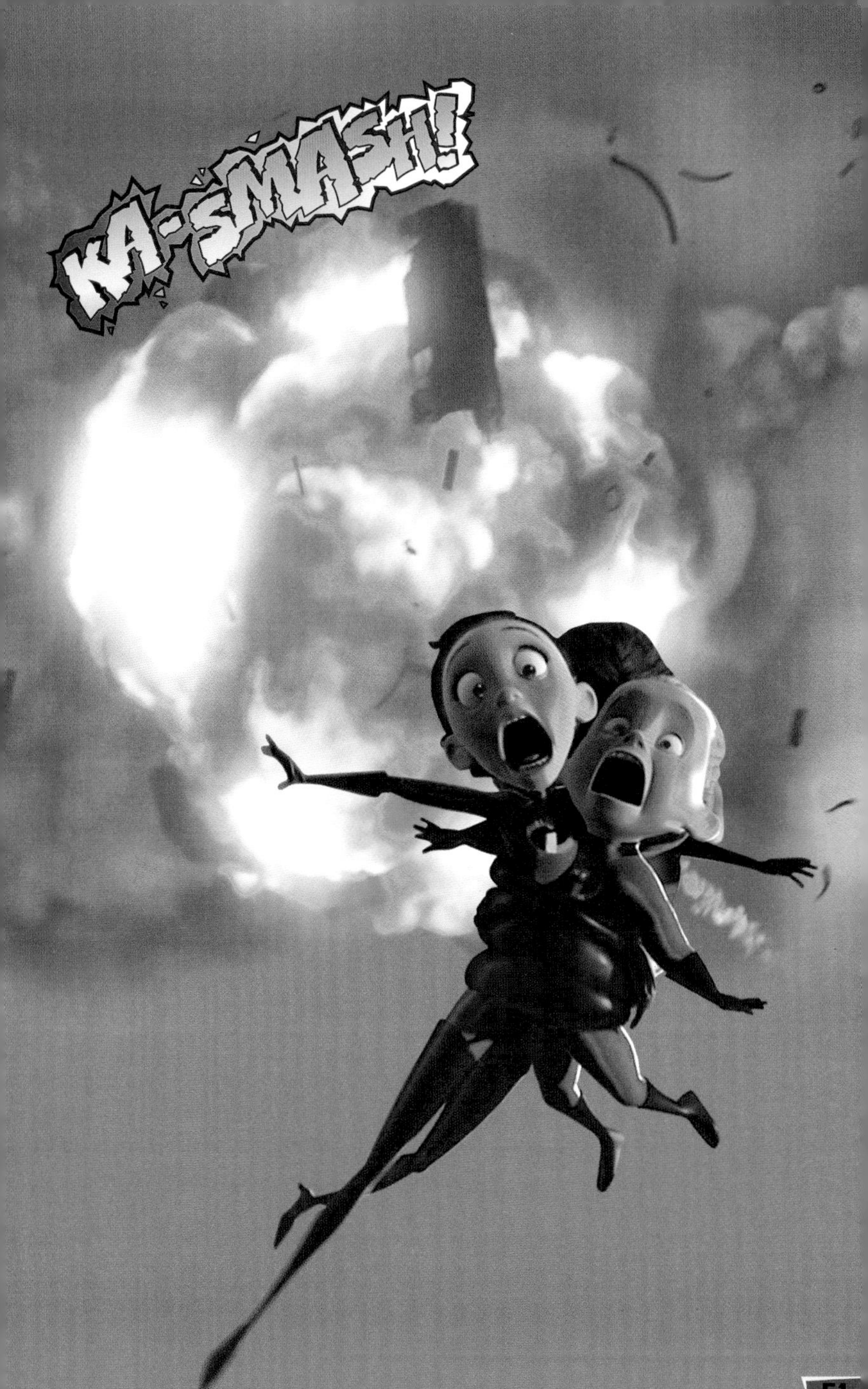
KA-SMASH!

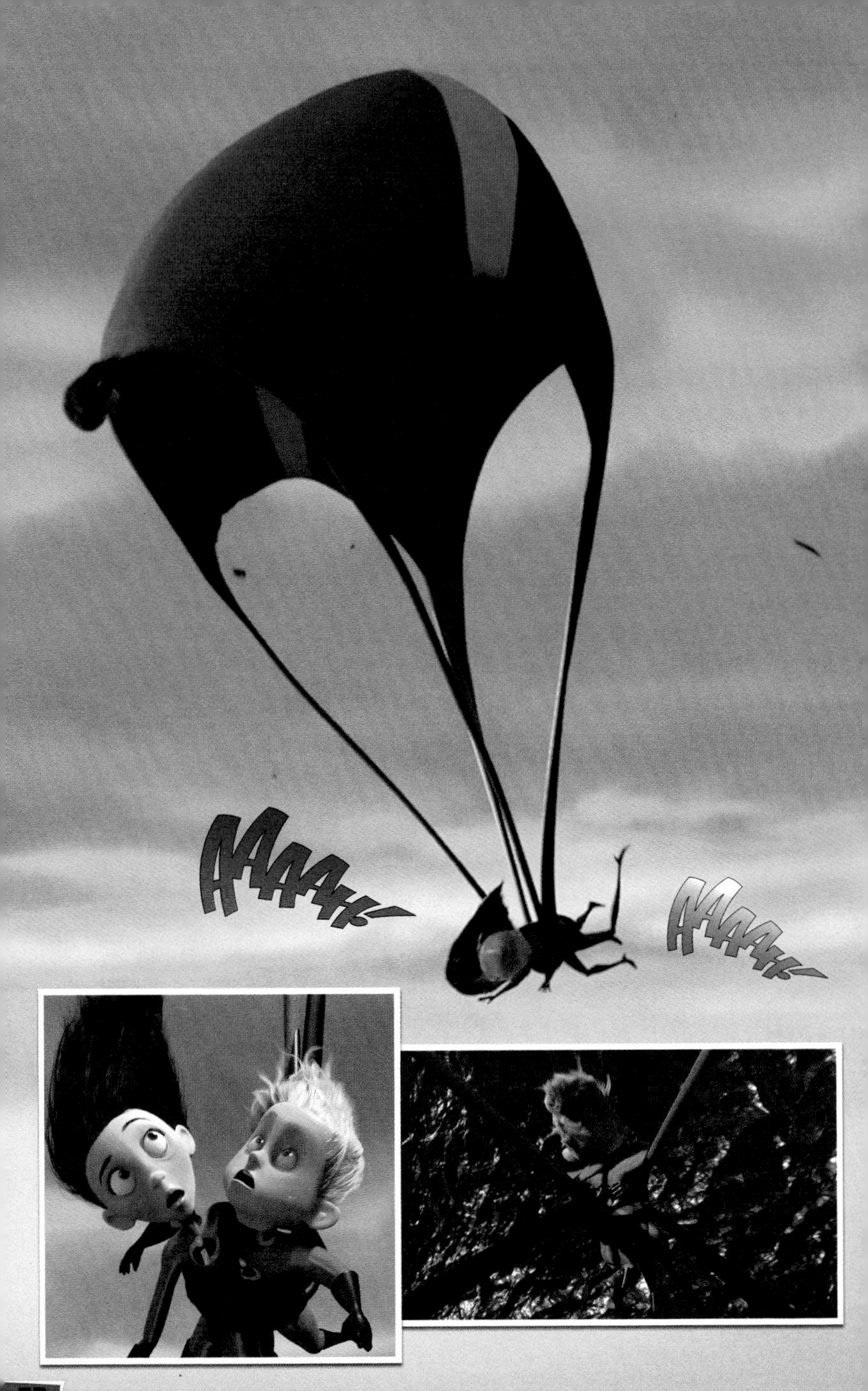
AAAAH!
AAAAH!

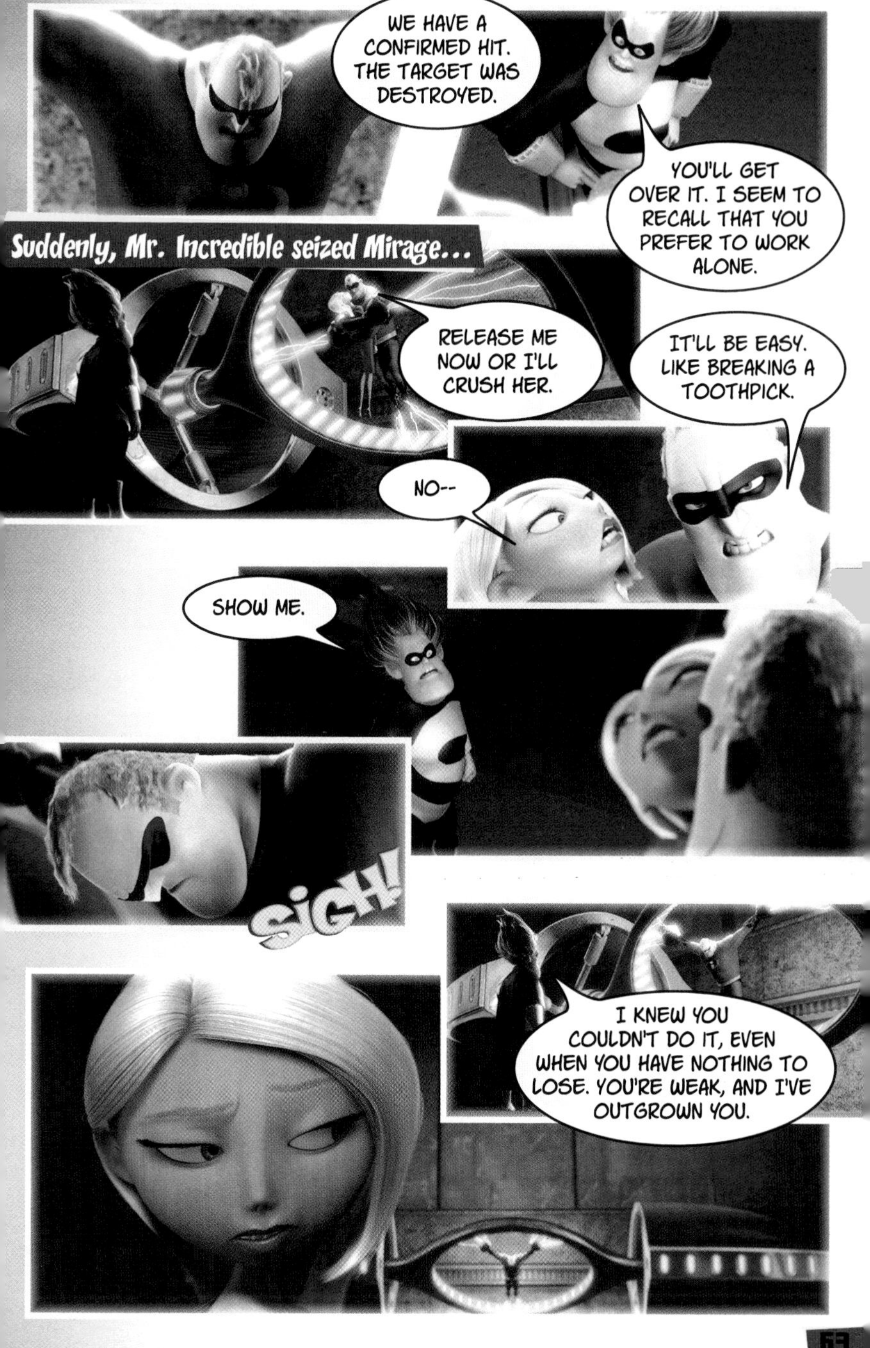
WE HAVE A CONFIRMED HIT. THE TARGET WAS DESTROYED.
YOU'LL GET OVER IT. I SEEM TO RECALL THAT YOU PREFER TO WORK ALONE.
Suddenly, Mr. Incredible seized Mirage...
RELEASE ME NOW OR I'LL CRUSH HER.
IT'LL BE EASY. LIKE BREAKING A TOOTHPICK.
NO--
SHOW ME.
SIGH!
I KNEW YOU COULDN'T DO IT, EVEN WHEN YOU HAVE NOTHING TO LOSE. YOU'RE WEAK, AND I'VE OUTGROWN YOU.

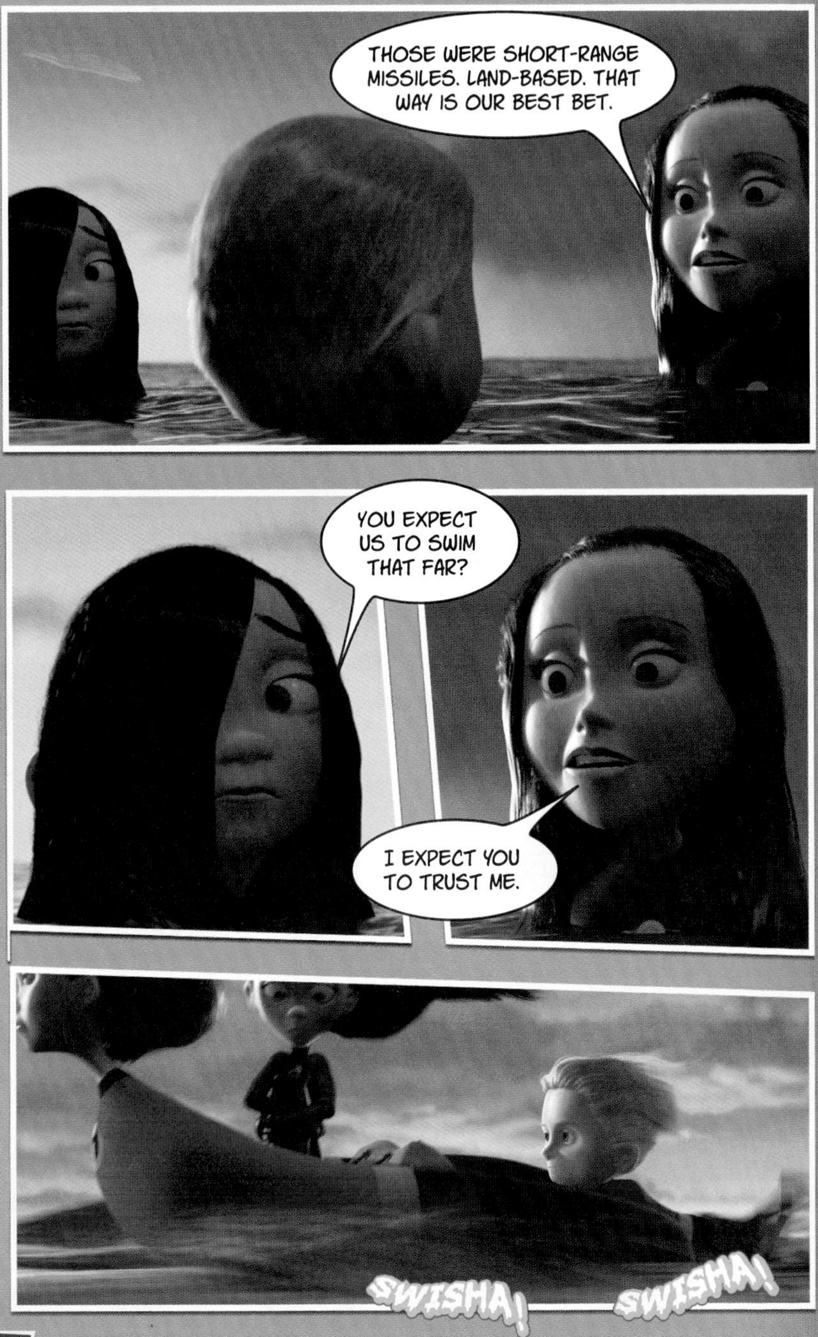
THOSE WERE SHORT-RANGE MISSILES. LAND-BASED. THAT WAY IS OUR BEST BET.
YOU EXPECT US TO SWIM THAT FAR?
I EXPECT YOU TO TRUST ME.
SWISHA!
SWISHA!

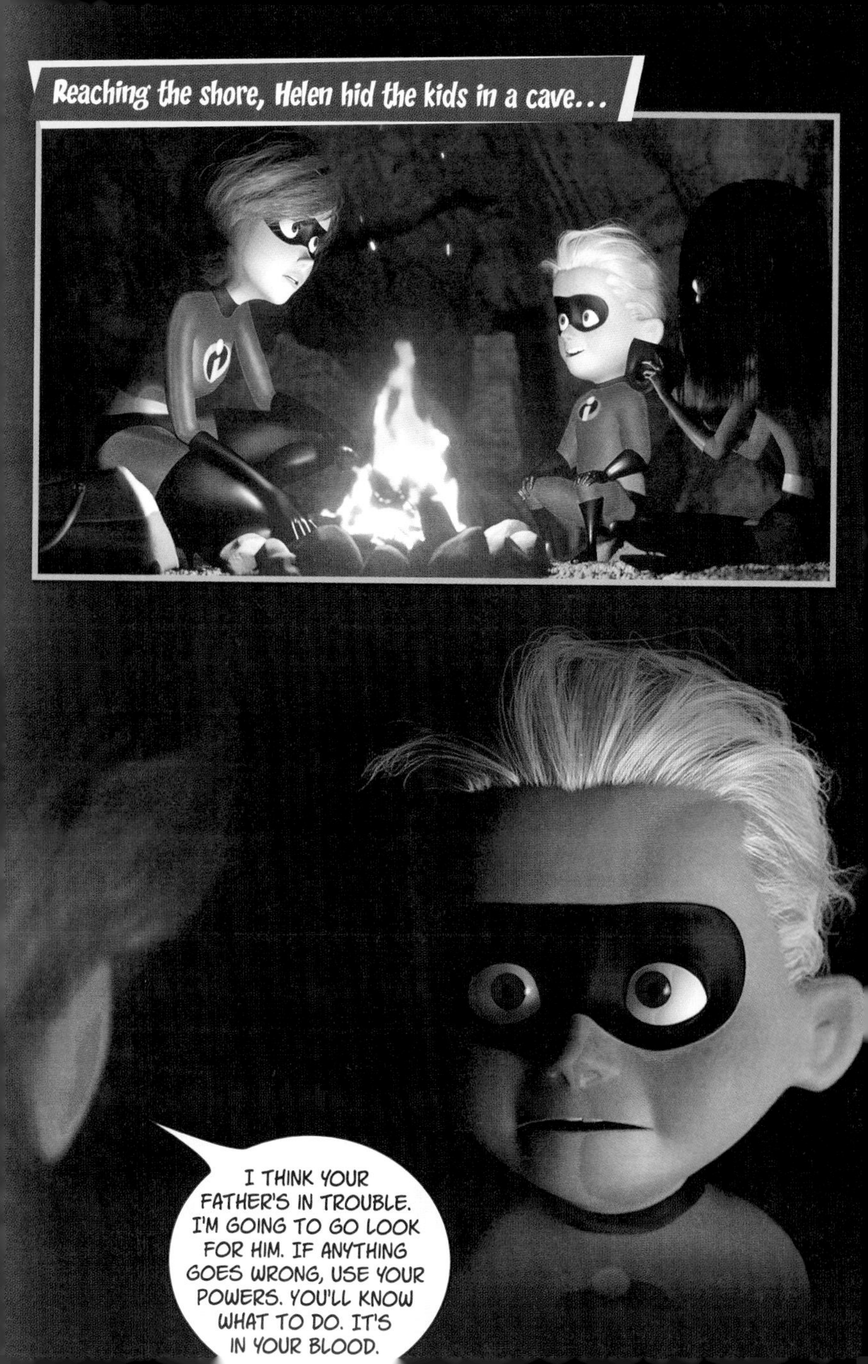
Reaching the shore, Helen hid the kids in a cave...
I THINK YOUR FATHER'S IN TROUBLE. I'M GOING TO GO LOOK FOR HIM. IF ANYTHING GOES WRONG, USE YOUR POWERS. YOU'LL KNOW WHAT TO DO. IT'S IN YOUR BLOOD.

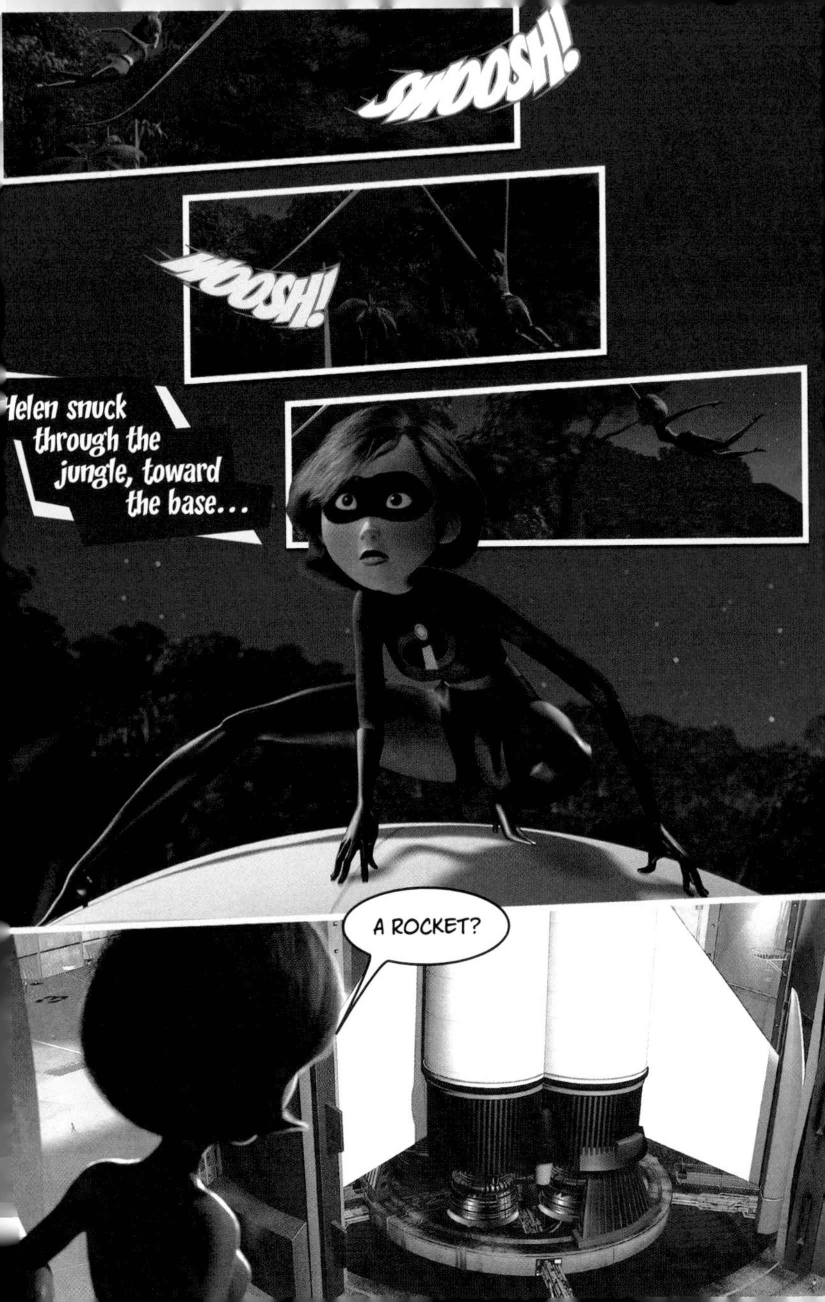
SHOOSH!
WHOOSH!
Helen snuck through the jungle, toward the base...
A ROCKET?

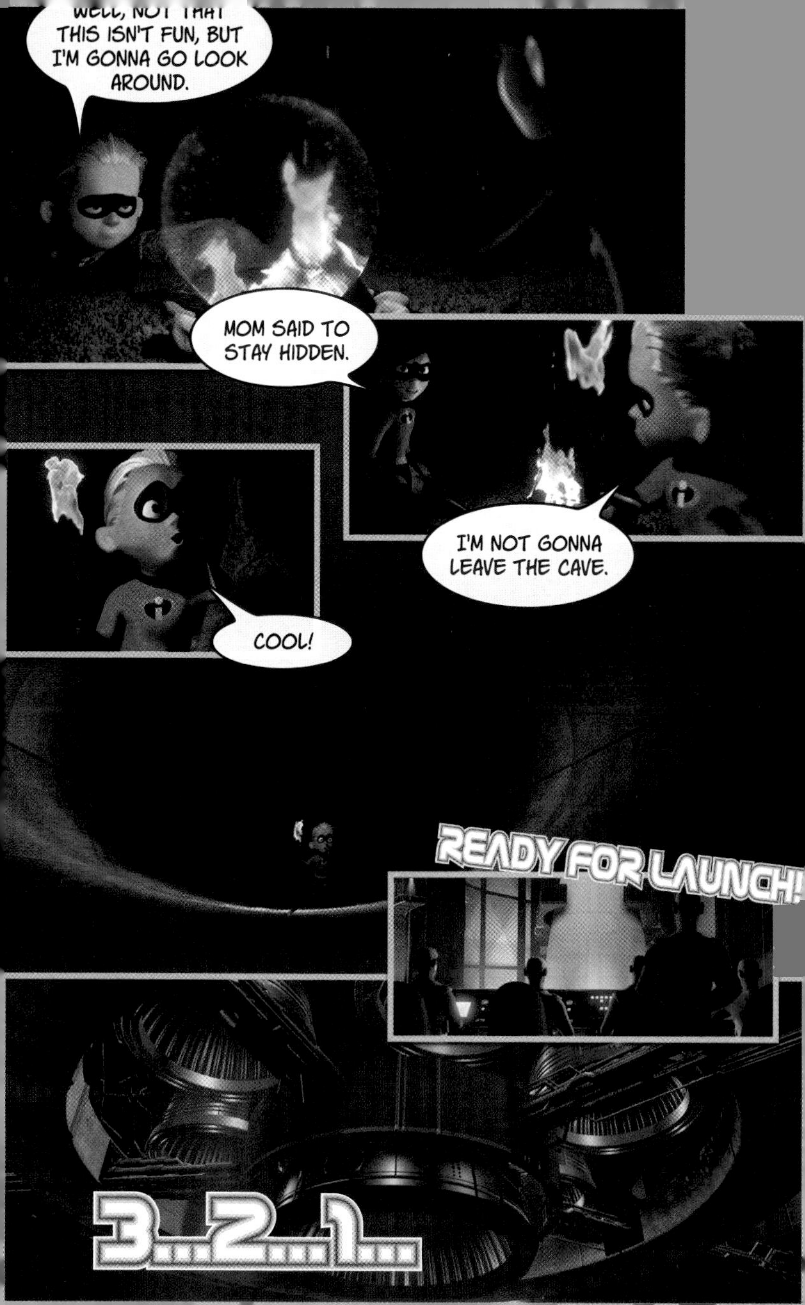

WELL, NOT THAT THIS ISN'T FUN, BUT I'M GONNA GO LOOK AROUND.
MOM SAID TO STAY HIDDEN.
I'M NOT GONNA LEAVE THE CAVE.
COOL!
READY FOR LAUNCH!
3...2...1...

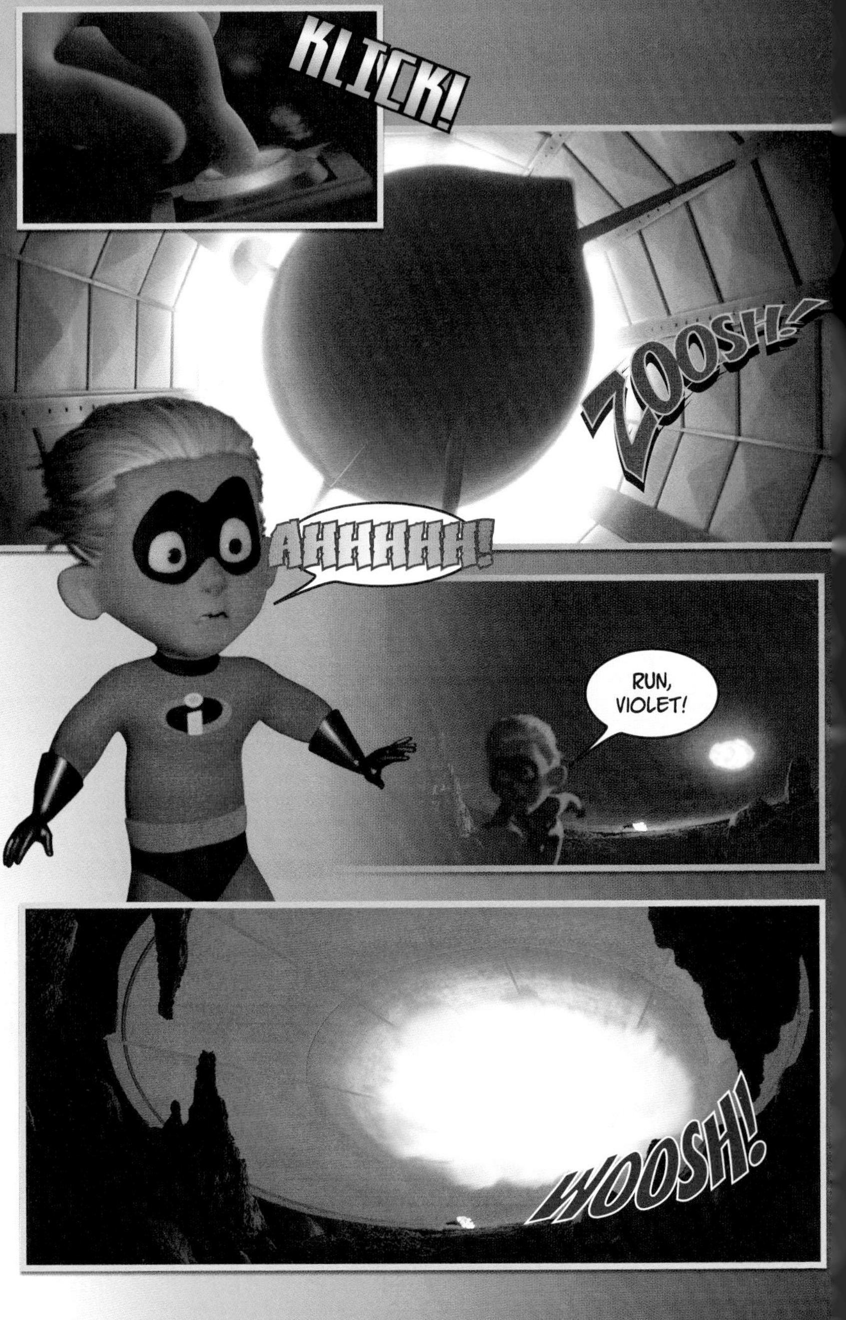
KLICK!
ZOOSH!
AHHHHH!
RUN, VIOLET!
WOOSH!

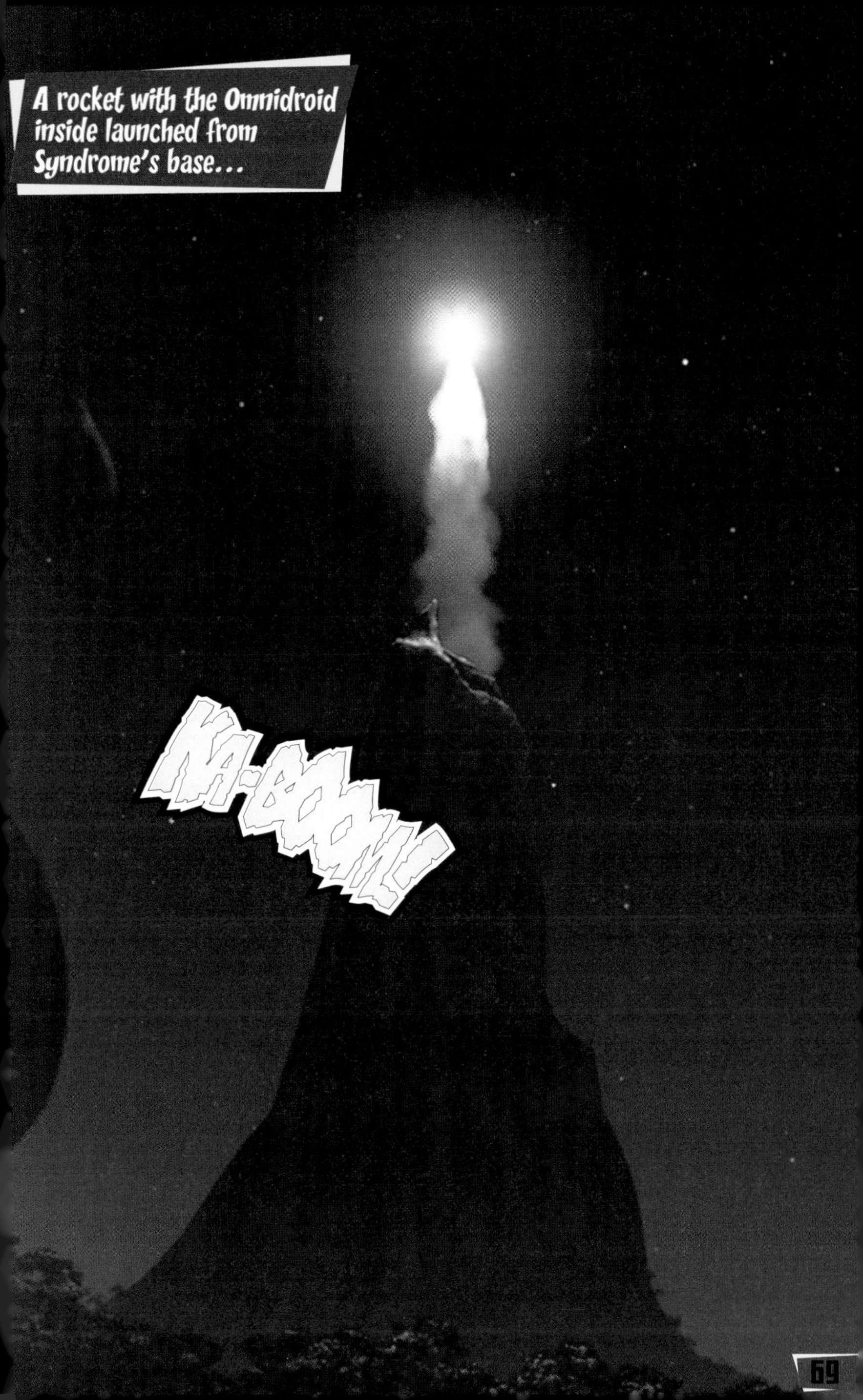
A rocket with the Omnidroid inside launched from Syndrome's base...
KA-BOOM!!

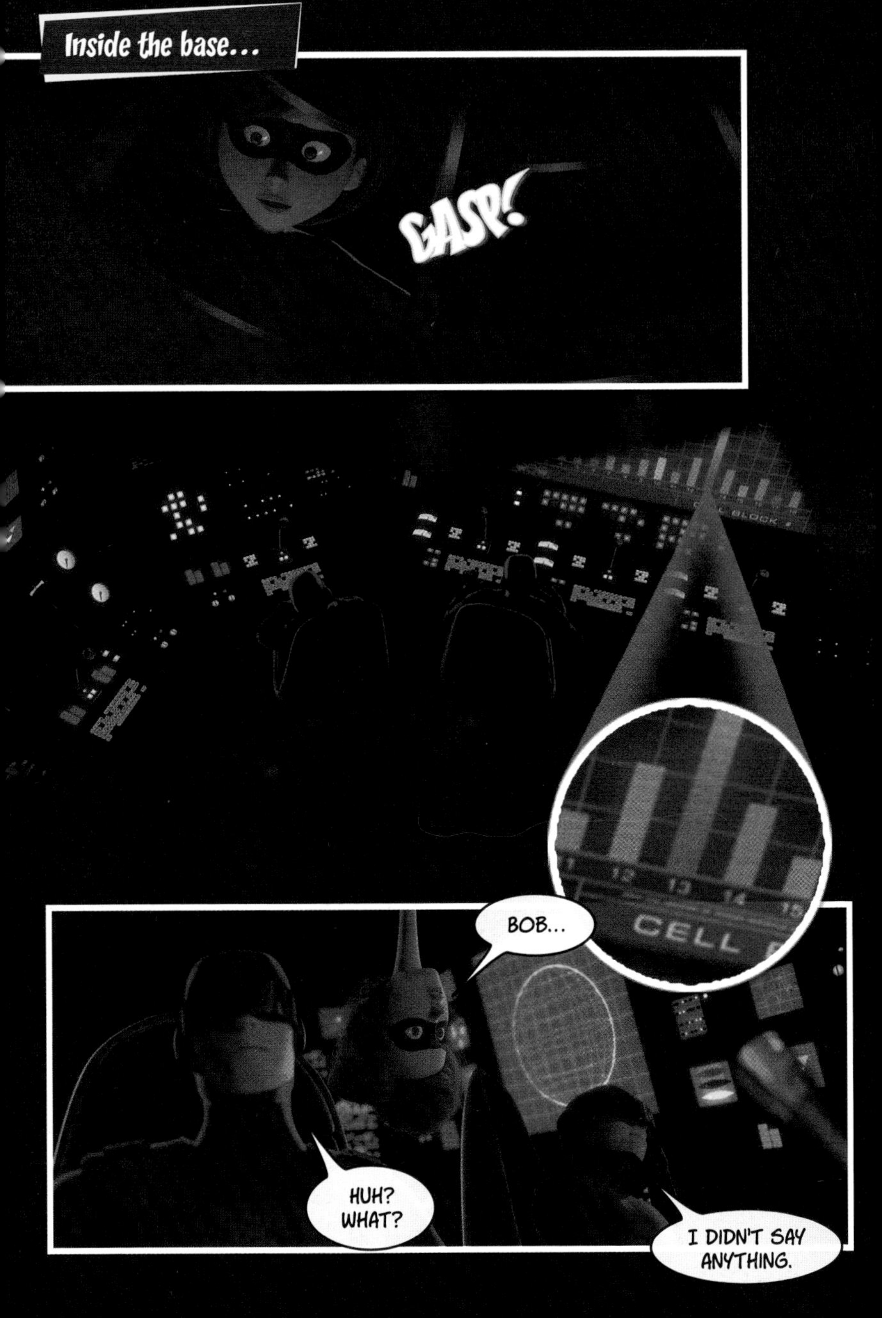
Inside the base...
GASP!
BOB...
HUH? WHAT?
I DIDN'T SAY ANYTHING.

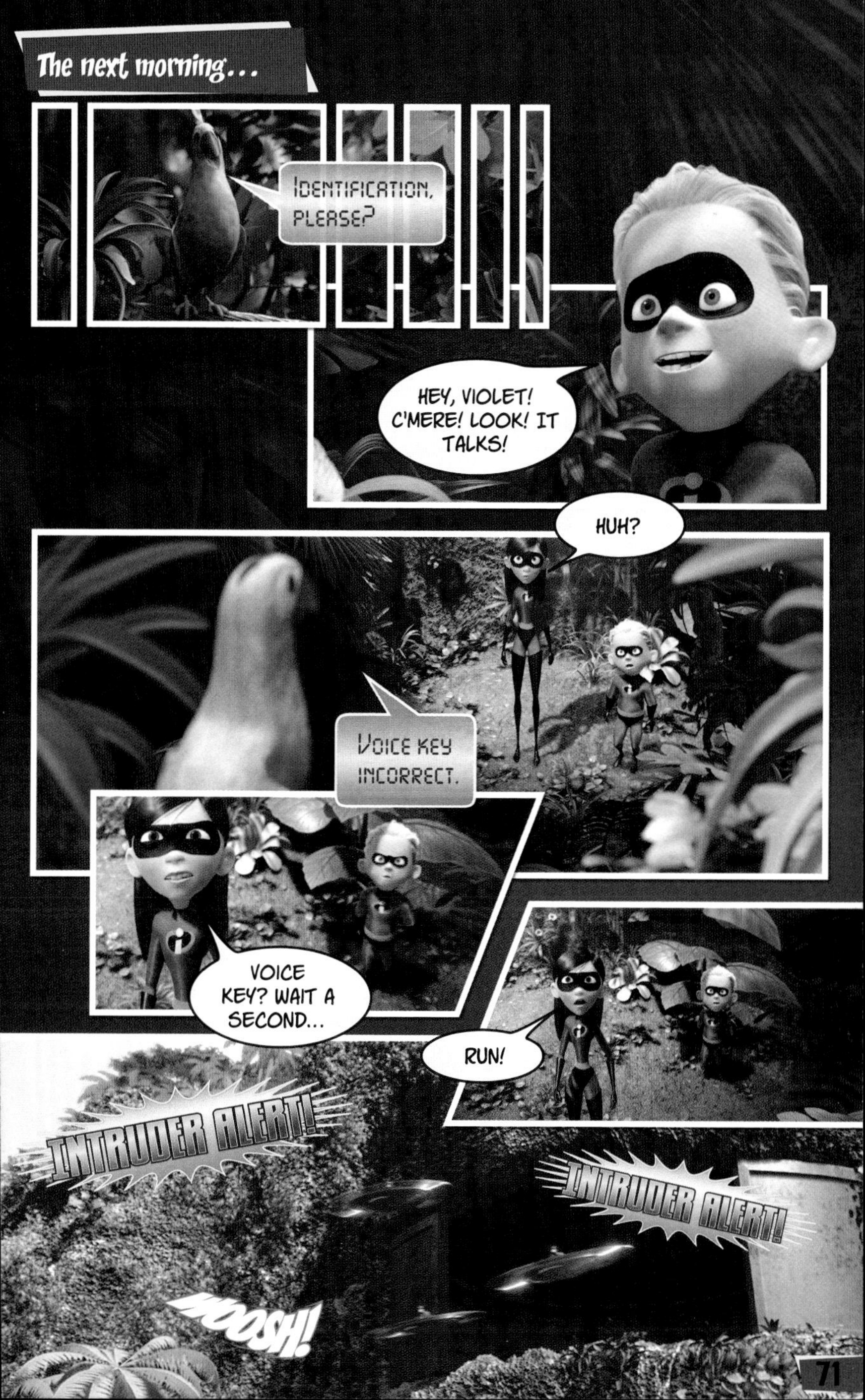
The next morning...
IDENTIFICATION, PLEASE?
HEY, VIOLET! C'MERE! LOOK! IT TALKS!
HUH?
VOICE KEY INCORRECT.
VOICE KEY? WAIT A SECOND...
RUN!
INTRUDER ALERT!
INTRUDER ALERT!
WHOOSH!

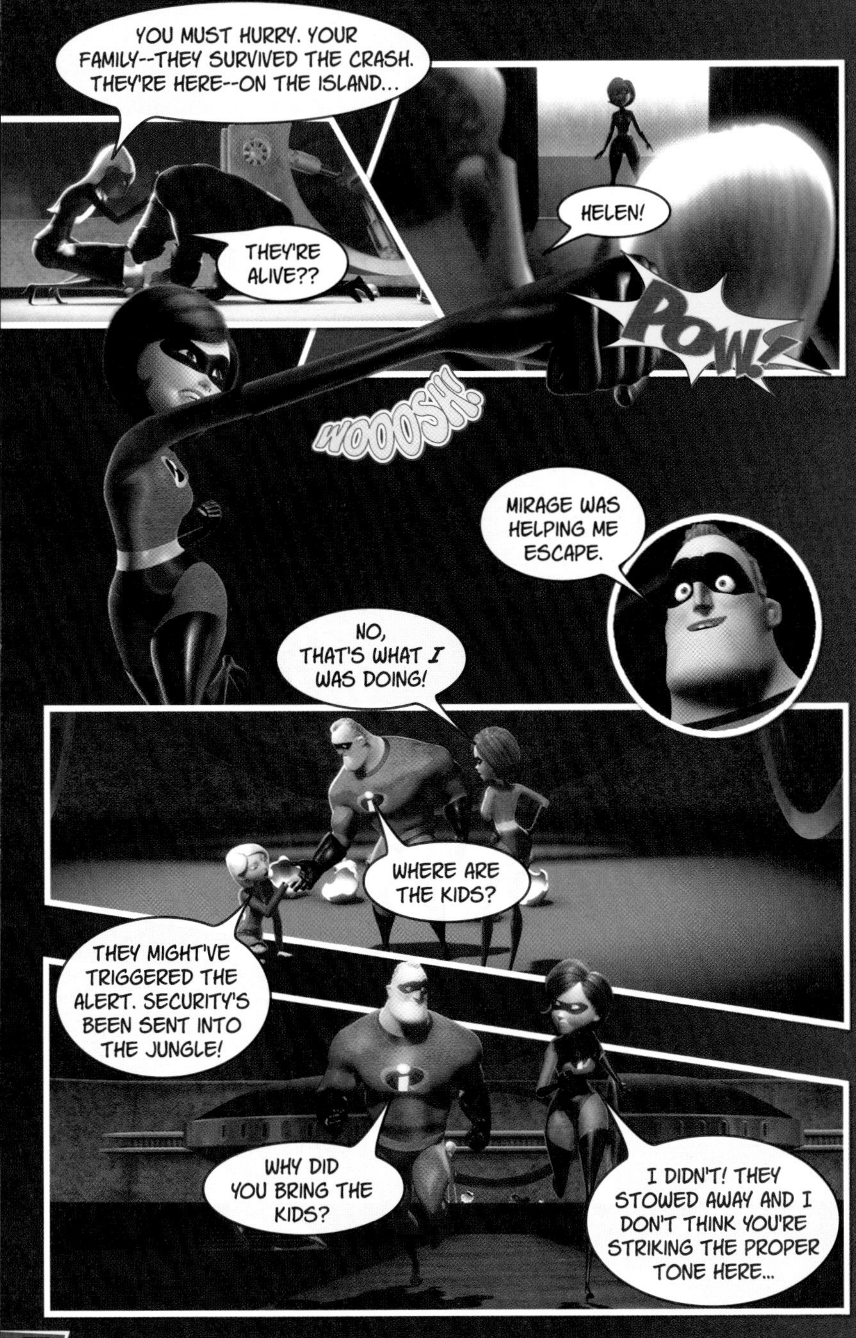

YOU MUST HURRY. YOUR FAMILY--THEY SURVIVED THE CRASH. THEY'RE HERE--ON THE ISLAND...
THEY'RE ALIVE??
HELEN!
POW!
WOOOSH!!
MIRAGE WAS HELPING ME ESCAPE.
NO, THAT'S WHAT *I* WAS DOING!
WHERE ARE THE KIDS?
THEY MIGHT'VE TRIGGERED THE ALERT. SECURITY'S BEEN SENT INTO THE JUNGLE!
WHY DID YOU BRING THE KIDS?
I DIDN'T! THEY STOWED AWAY AND I DON'T THINK YOU'RE STRIKING THE PROPER TONE HERE...

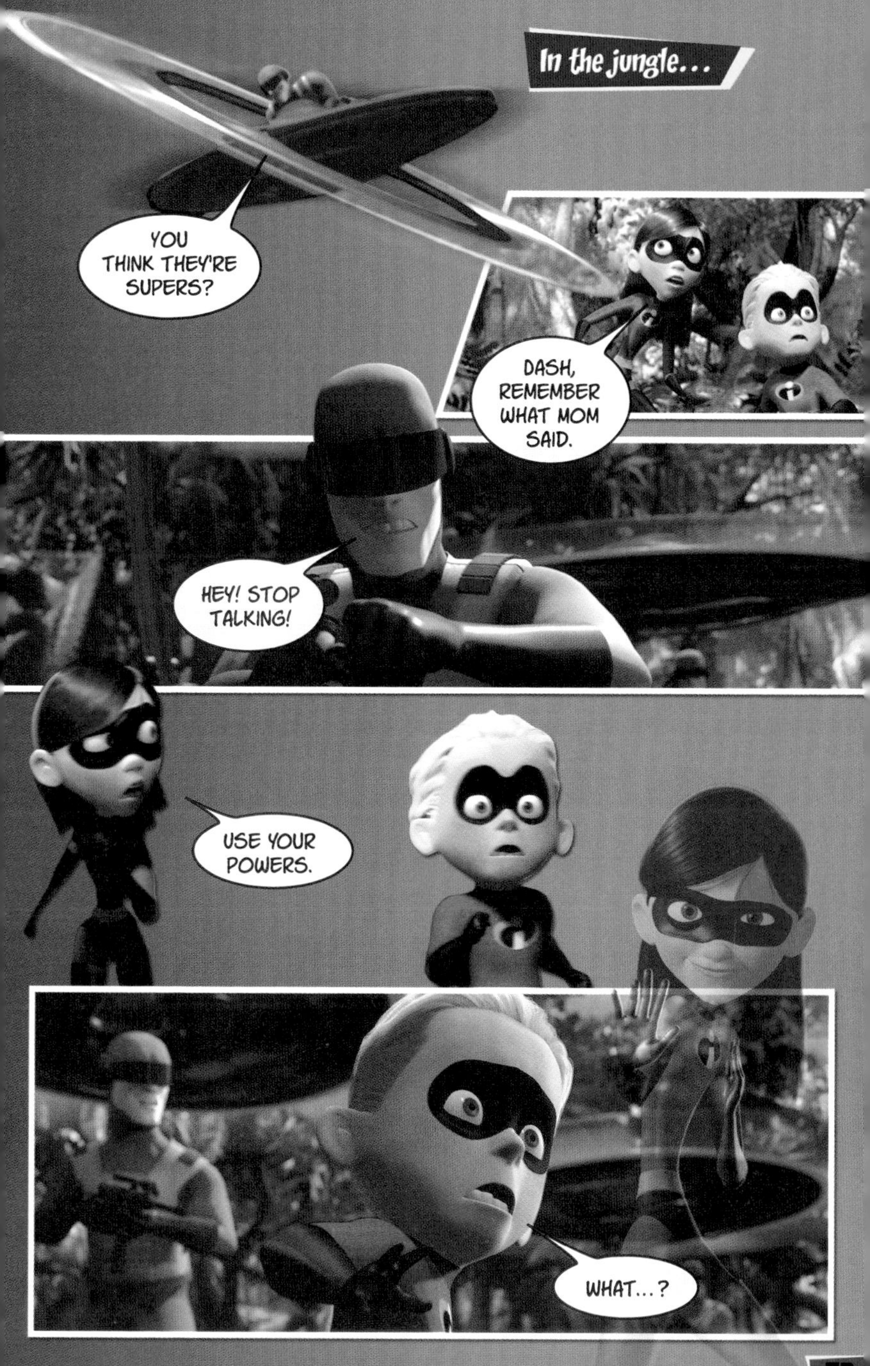
In the jungle...
YOU THINK THEY'RE SUPERS?
DASH, REMEMBER WHAT MOM SAID.
HEY! STOP TALKING!
USE YOUR POWERS.
WHAT...?

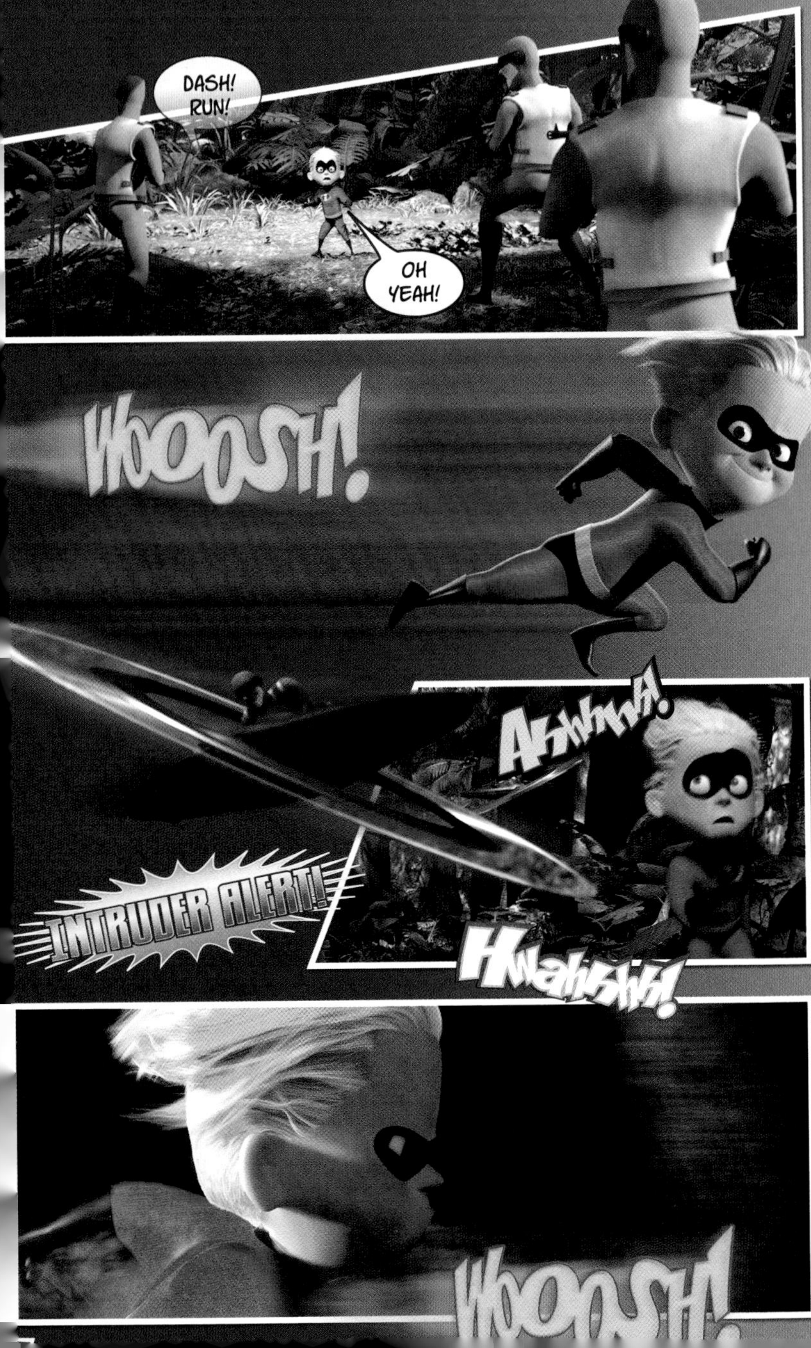
DASH! RUN!
OH YEAH!
WOOOSH!
AHHHWA!
INTRUDER ALERT!
HWAHHWA!
WOOOSH!

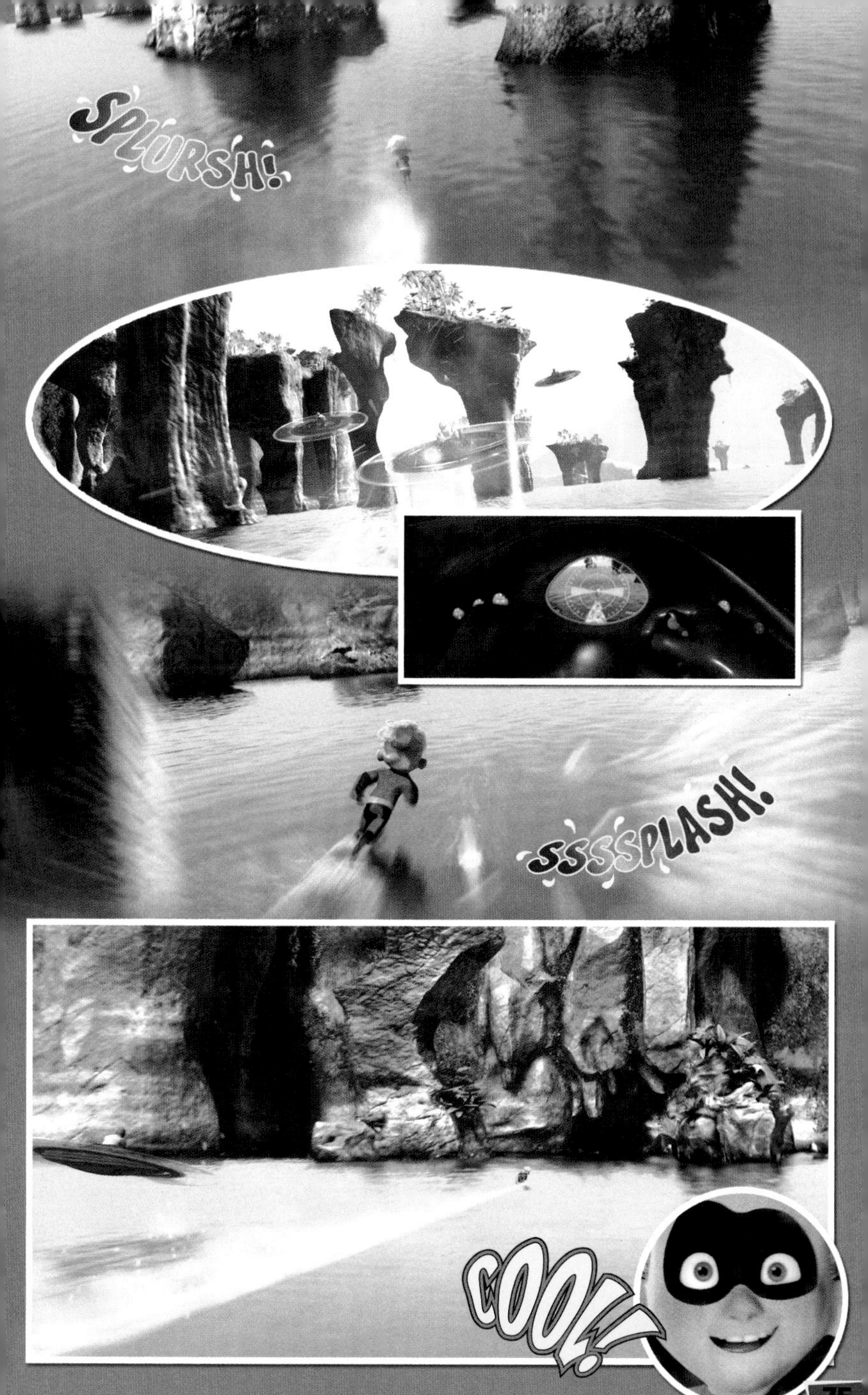
SPLURSH!
SSSSPLASH!
COOL!

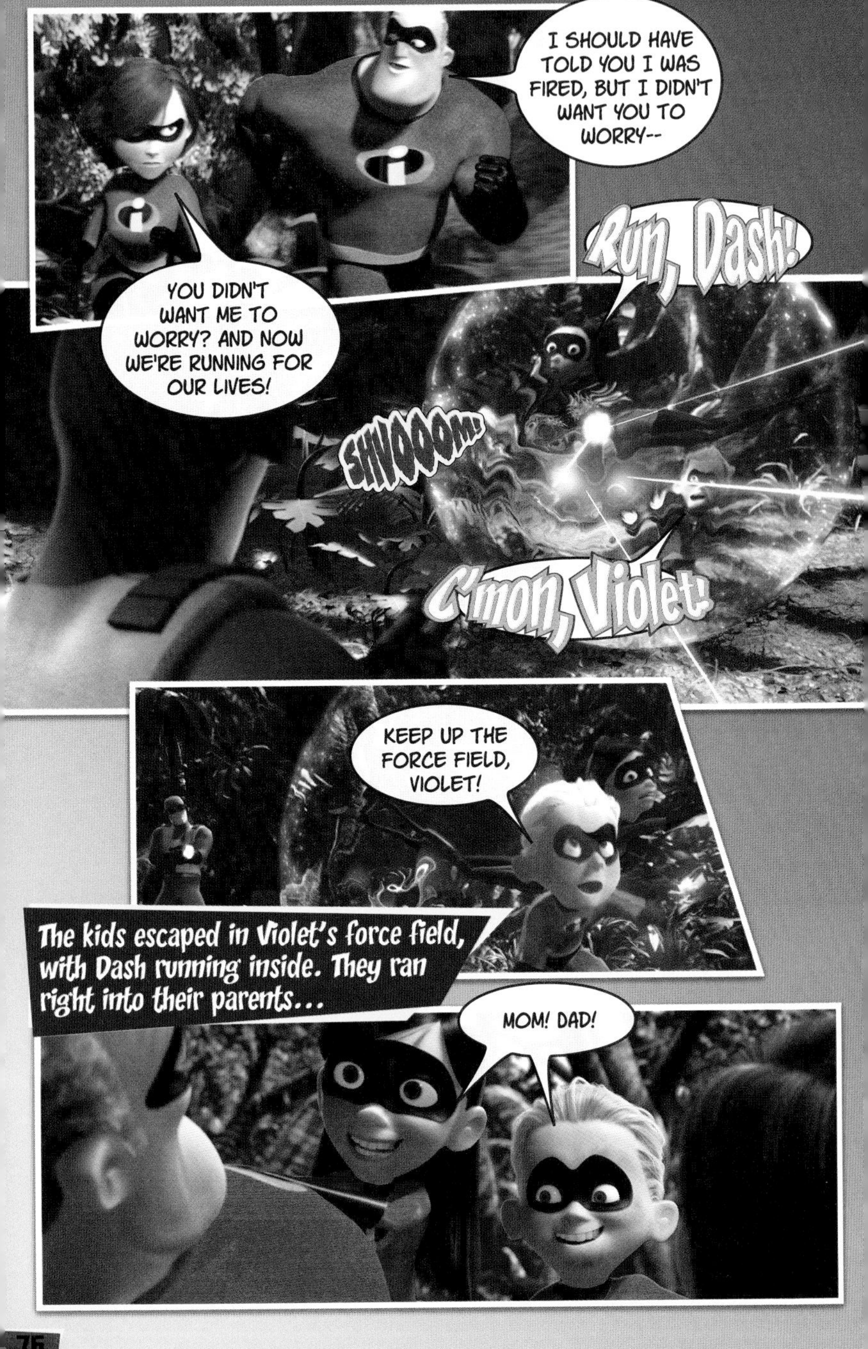
I SHOULD HAVE TOLD YOU I WAS FIRED, BUT I DIDN'T WANT YOU TO WORRY--
YOU DIDN'T WANT ME TO WORRY? AND NOW WE'RE RUNNING FOR OUR LIVES!
Run, Dash!
SHVOOOM!
C'mon, Violet!
KEEP UP THE FORCE FIELD, VIOLET!
The kids escaped in Violet's force field, with Dash running inside. They ran right into their parents...
MOM! DAD!

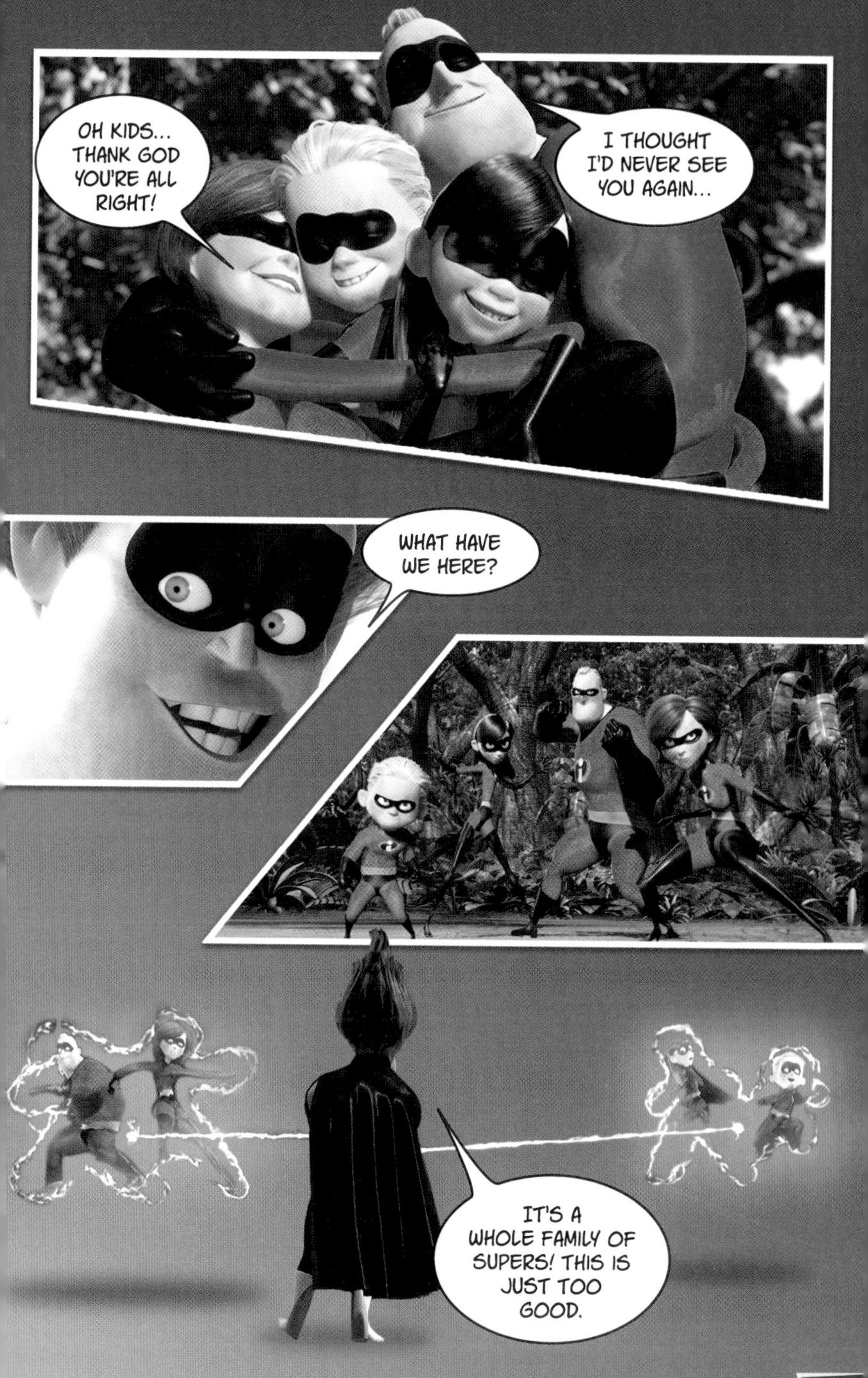
OH KIDS... THANK GOD YOU'RE ALL RIGHT!
I THOUGHT I'D NEVER SEE YOU AGAIN...
WHAT HAVE WE HERE?
IT'S A WHOLE FAMILY OF SUPERS! THIS IS JUST TOO GOOD.

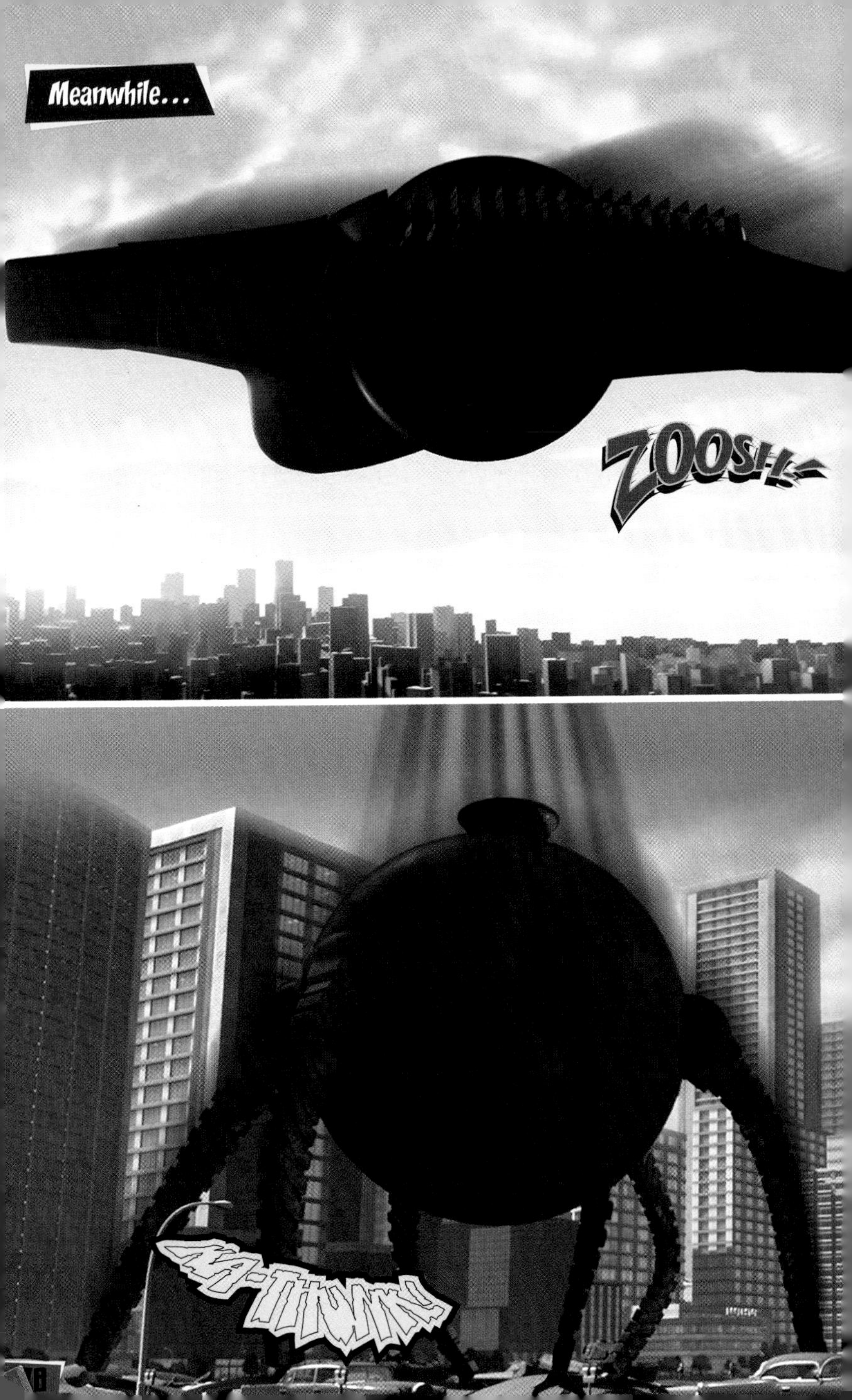
Meanwhile...
ZOOSH!
KA-THUNK!

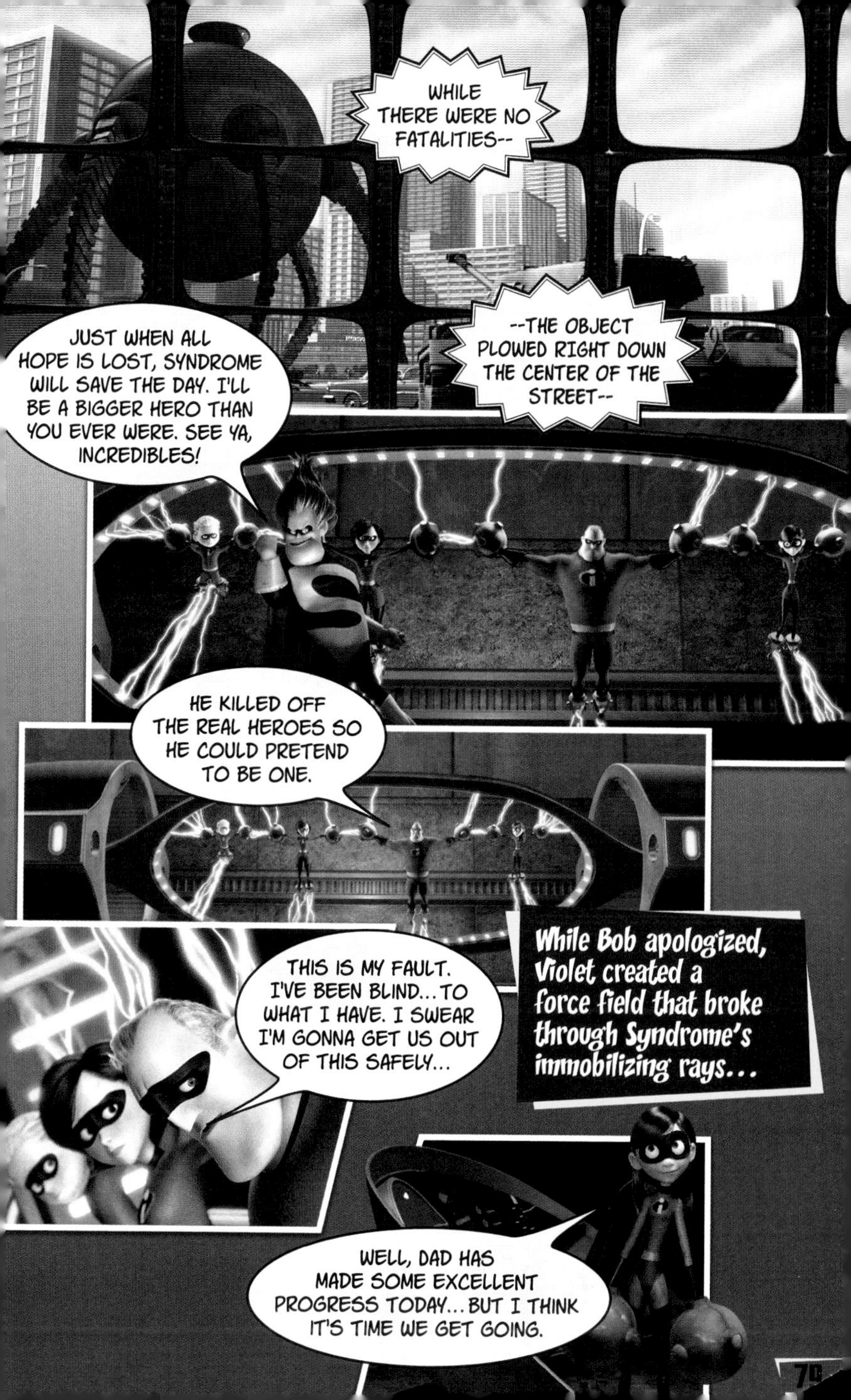
WHILE THERE WERE NO FATALITIES--
JUST WHEN ALL HOPE IS LOST, SYNDROME WILL SAVE THE DAY. I'LL BE A BIGGER HERO THAN YOU EVER WERE. SEE YA, INCREDIBLES!
--THE OBJECT PLOWED RIGHT DOWN THE CENTER OF THE STREET--
HE KILLED OFF THE REAL HEROES SO HE COULD PRETEND TO BE ONE.
THIS IS MY FAULT. I'VE BEEN BLIND... TO WHAT I HAVE. I SWEAR I'M GONNA GET US OUT OF THIS SAFELY...
While Bob apologized, Violet created a force field that broke through Syndrome's immobilizing rays...
WELL, DAD HAS MADE SOME EXCELLENT PROGRESS TODAY... BUT I THINK IT'S TIME WE GET GOING.

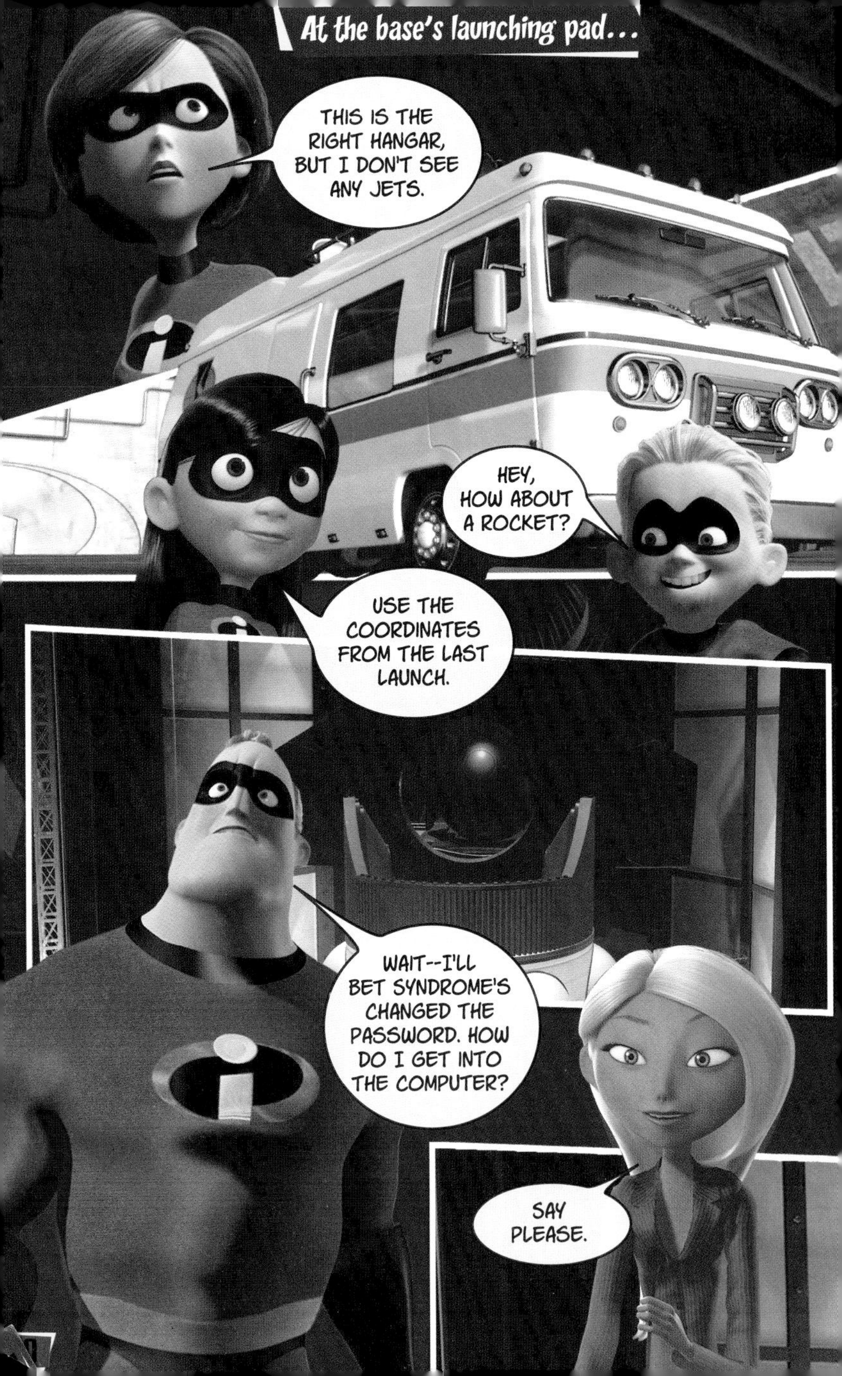

At the base's launching pad...
THIS IS THE RIGHT HANGAR, BUT I DON'T SEE ANY JETS.
HEY, HOW ABOUT A ROCKET?
USE THE COORDINATES FROM THE LAST LAUNCH.
WAIT--I'LL BET SYNDROME'S CHANGED THE PASSWORD. HOW DO I GET INTO THE COMPUTER?
SAY PLEASE.

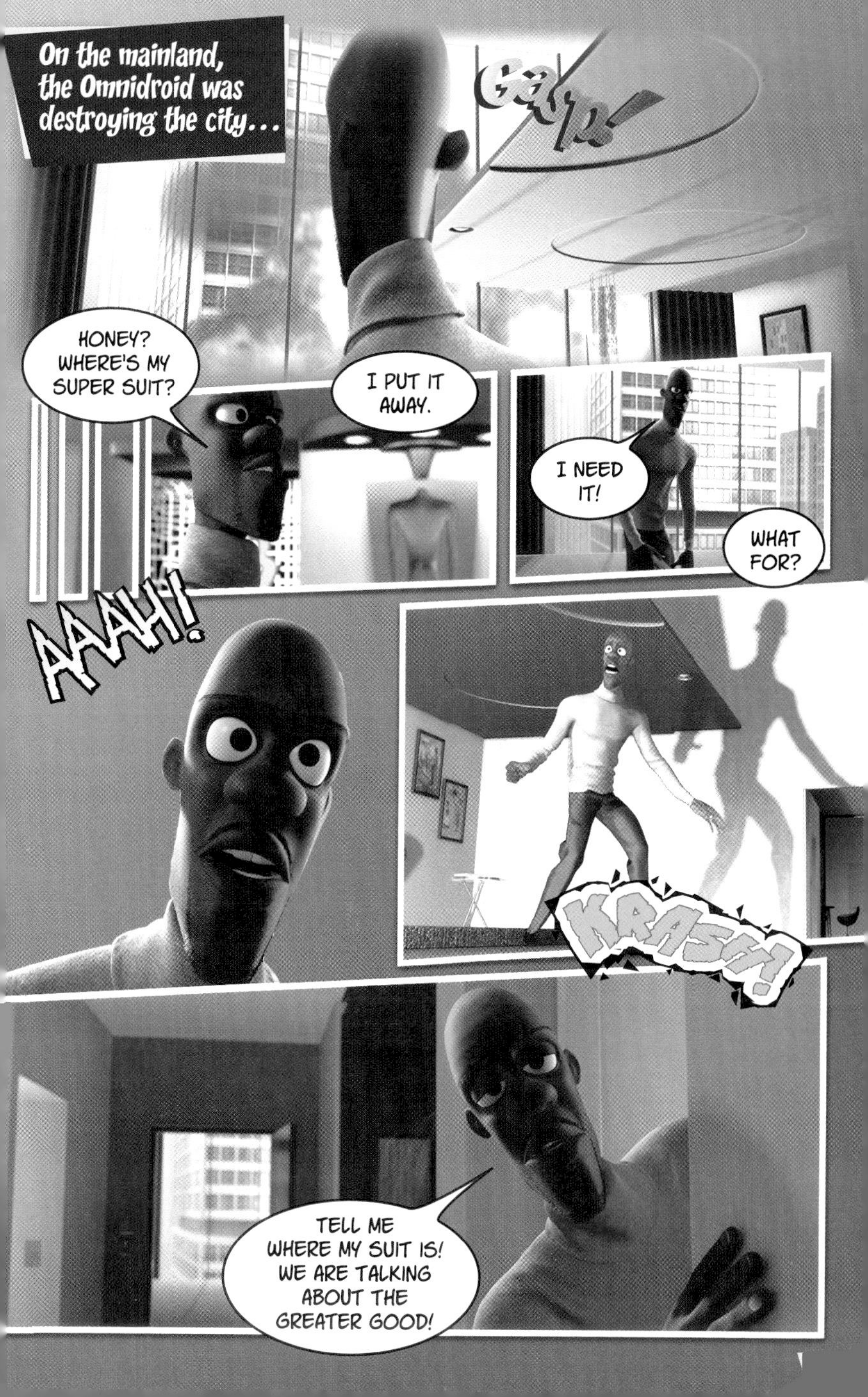

On the mainland, the Omnidroid was destroying the city...
GASP!
HONEY? WHERE'S MY SUPER SUIT?
I PUT IT AWAY.
I NEED IT!
WHAT FOR?
AAAH!
KRASH!
TELL ME WHERE MY SUIT IS! WE ARE TALKING ABOUT THE GREATER GOOD!

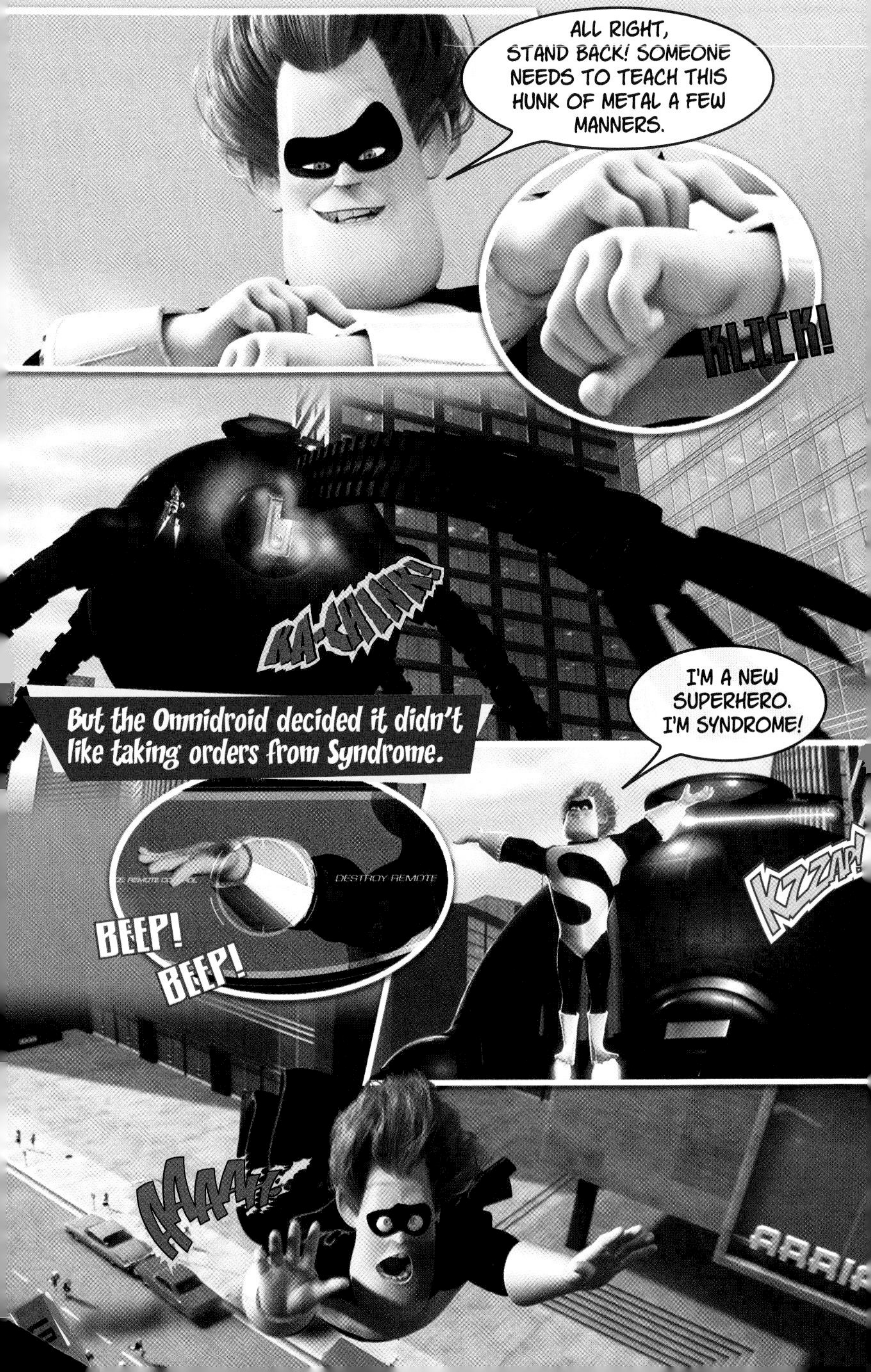
ALL RIGHT, STAND BACK! SOMEONE NEEDS TO TEACH THIS HUNK OF METAL A FEW MANNERS.
KLICK!
KA-CHINK!
But the Omnidroid decided it didn't like taking orders from Syndrome.
DESTROY REMOTE
BEEP! BEEP!
I'M A NEW SUPERHERO. I'M SYNDROME!
KZZAP!
AAAAH!

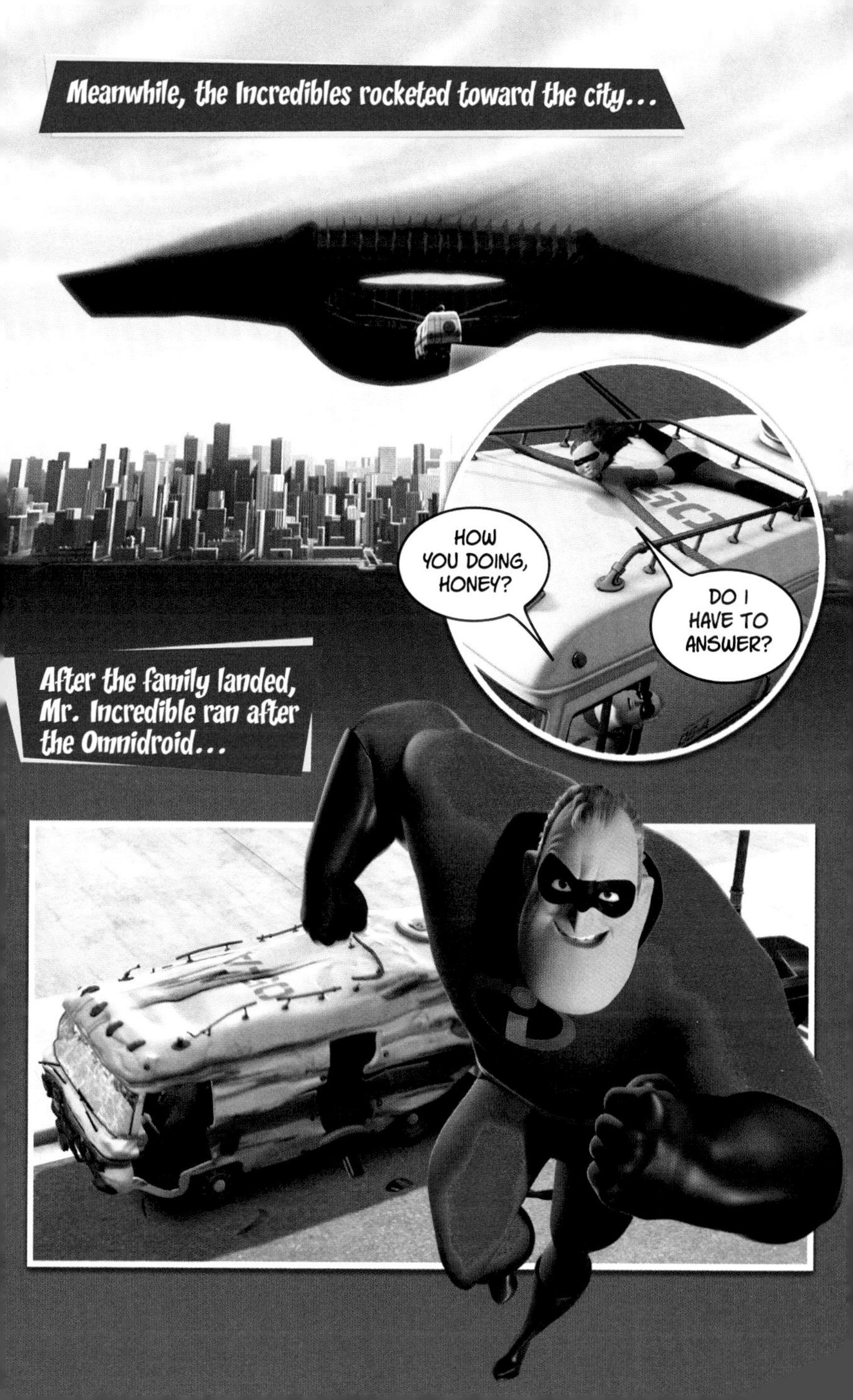
Meanwhile, the Incredibles rocketed toward the city...
HOW YOU DOING, HONEY?
DO I HAVE TO ANSWER?
After the family landed, Mr. Incredible ran after the Omnidroid...

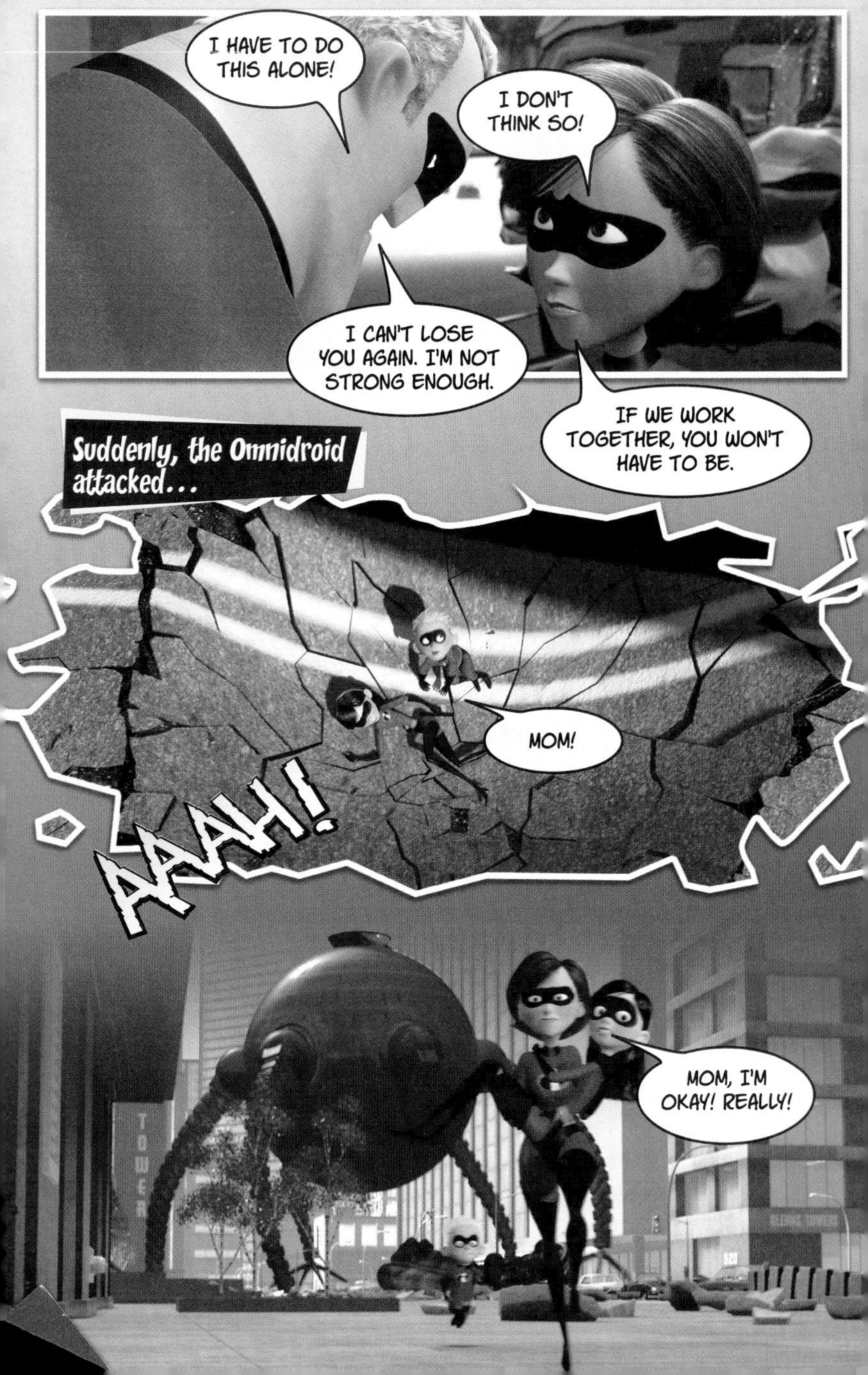
I HAVE TO DO THIS ALONE!
I DON'T THINK SO!
I CAN'T LOSE YOU AGAIN. I'M NOT STRONG ENOUGH.
IF WE WORK TOGETHER, YOU WON'T HAVE TO BE.
Suddenly, the Omnidroid attacked...
MOM!
AAAH!
MOM, I'M OKAY! REALLY!

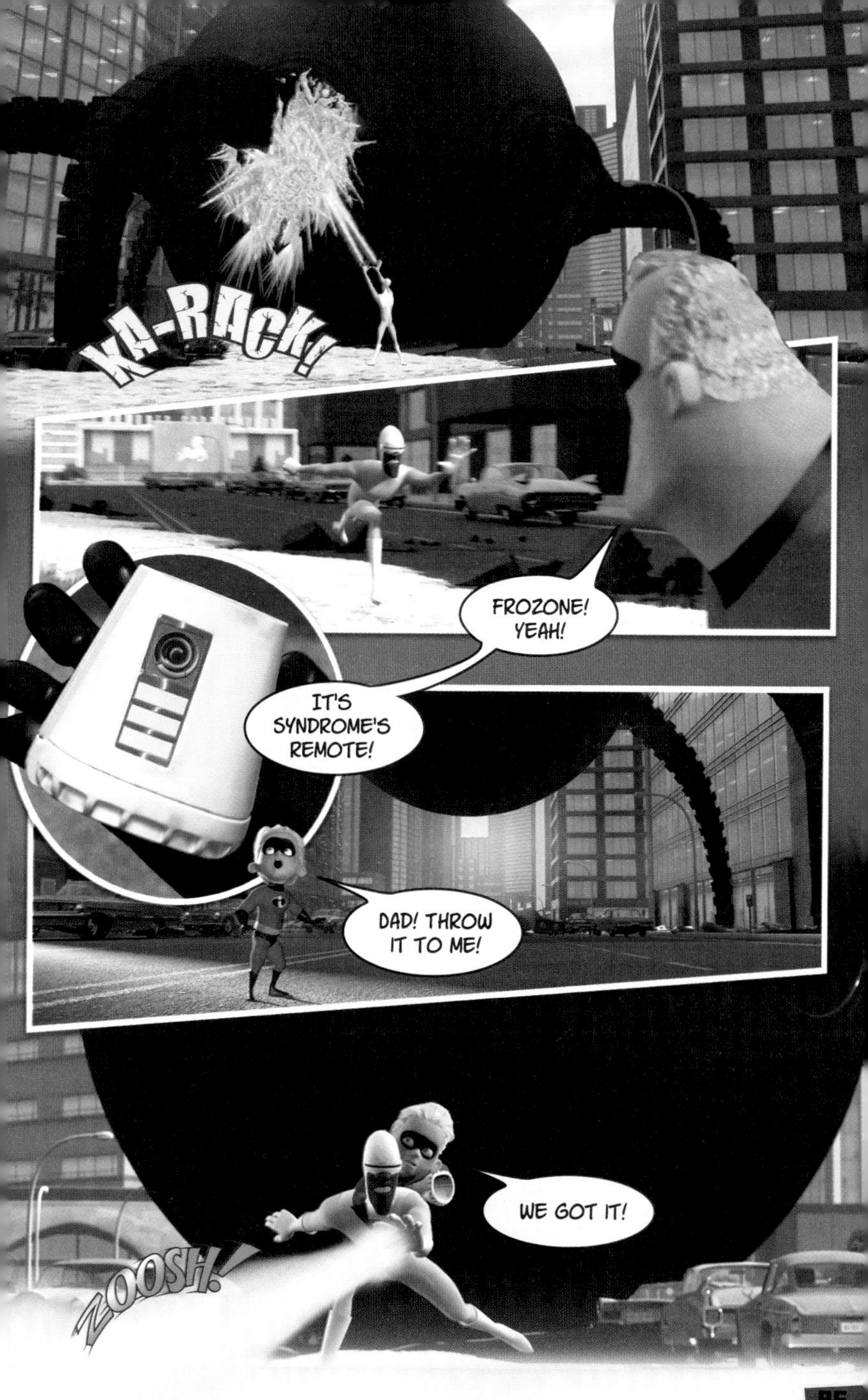
KA-RACK!
FROZONE! YEAH!
IT'S SYNDROME'S REMOTE!
DAD! THROW IT TO ME!
WE GOT IT!
ZOOSH!

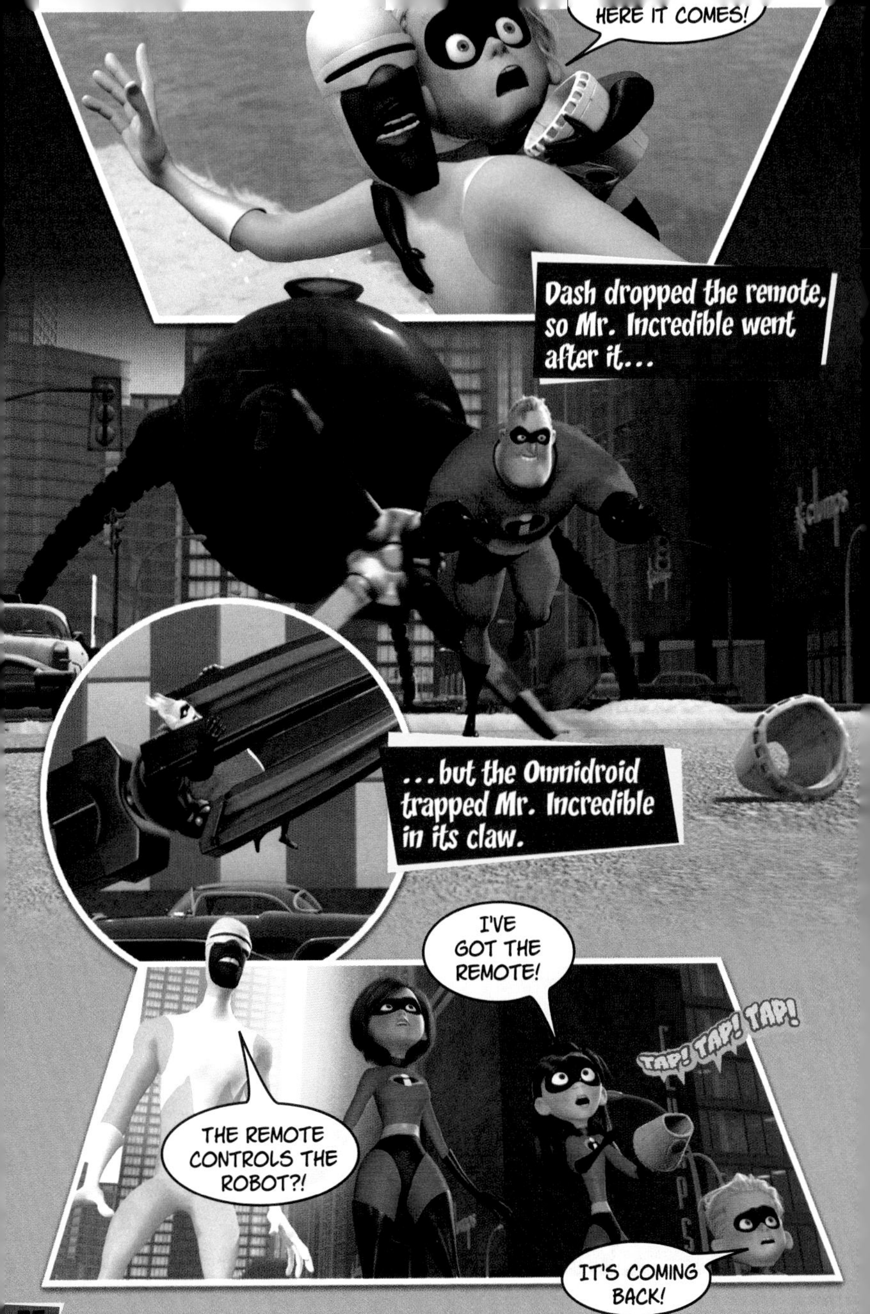
HERE IT COMES!
Dash dropped the remote, so Mr. Incredible went after it...
...but the Omnidroid trapped Mr. Incredible in its claw.
I'VE GOT THE REMOTE!
TAP! TAP! TAP!
THE REMOTE CONTROLS THE ROBOT?!
IT'S COMING BACK!

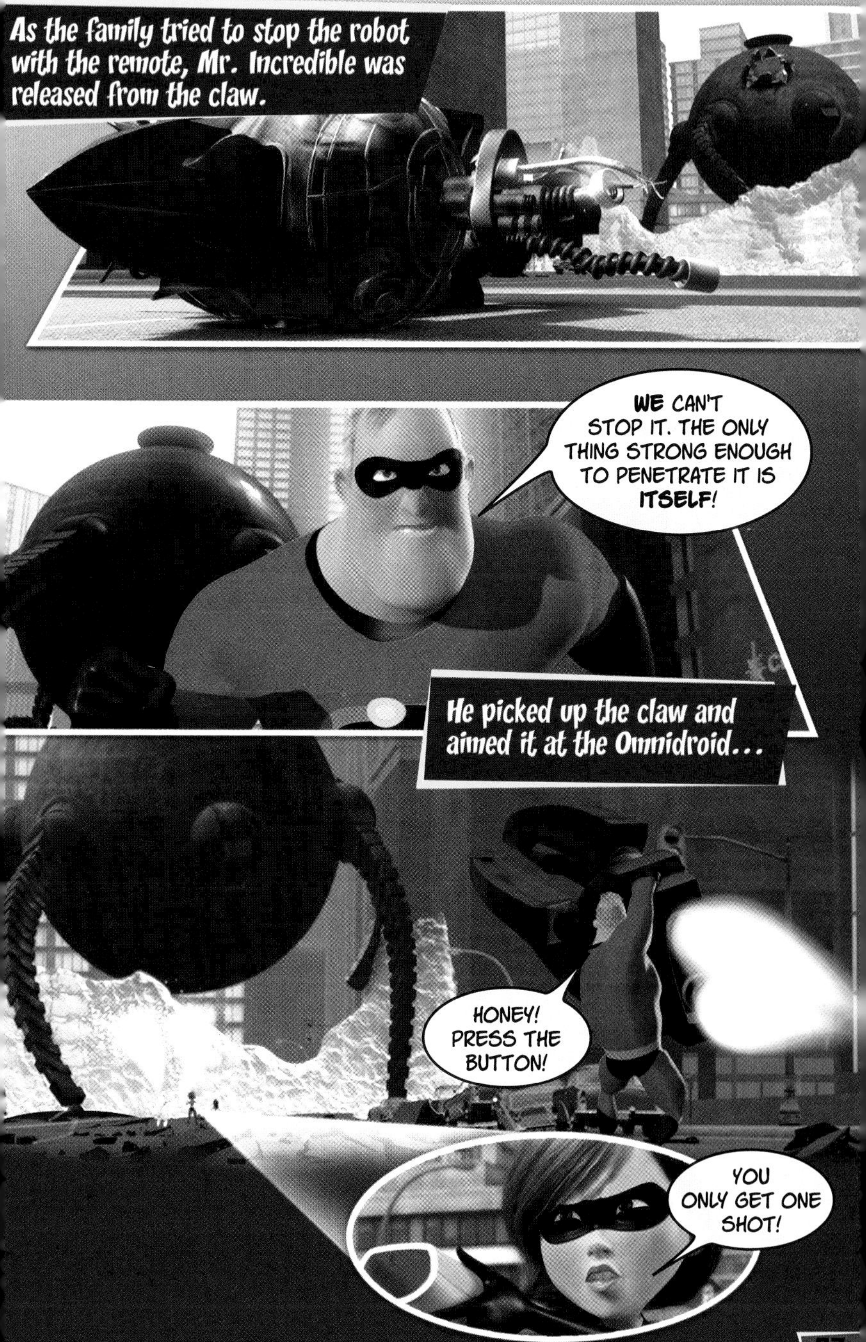

As the family tried to stop the robot with the remote, Mr. Incredible was released from the claw.
WE CAN'T STOP IT. THE ONLY THING STRONG ENOUGH TO PENETRATE IT IS ITSELF!
He picked up the claw and aimed it at the Omnidroid...
HONEY! PRESS THE BUTTON!
YOU ONLY GET ONE SHOT!

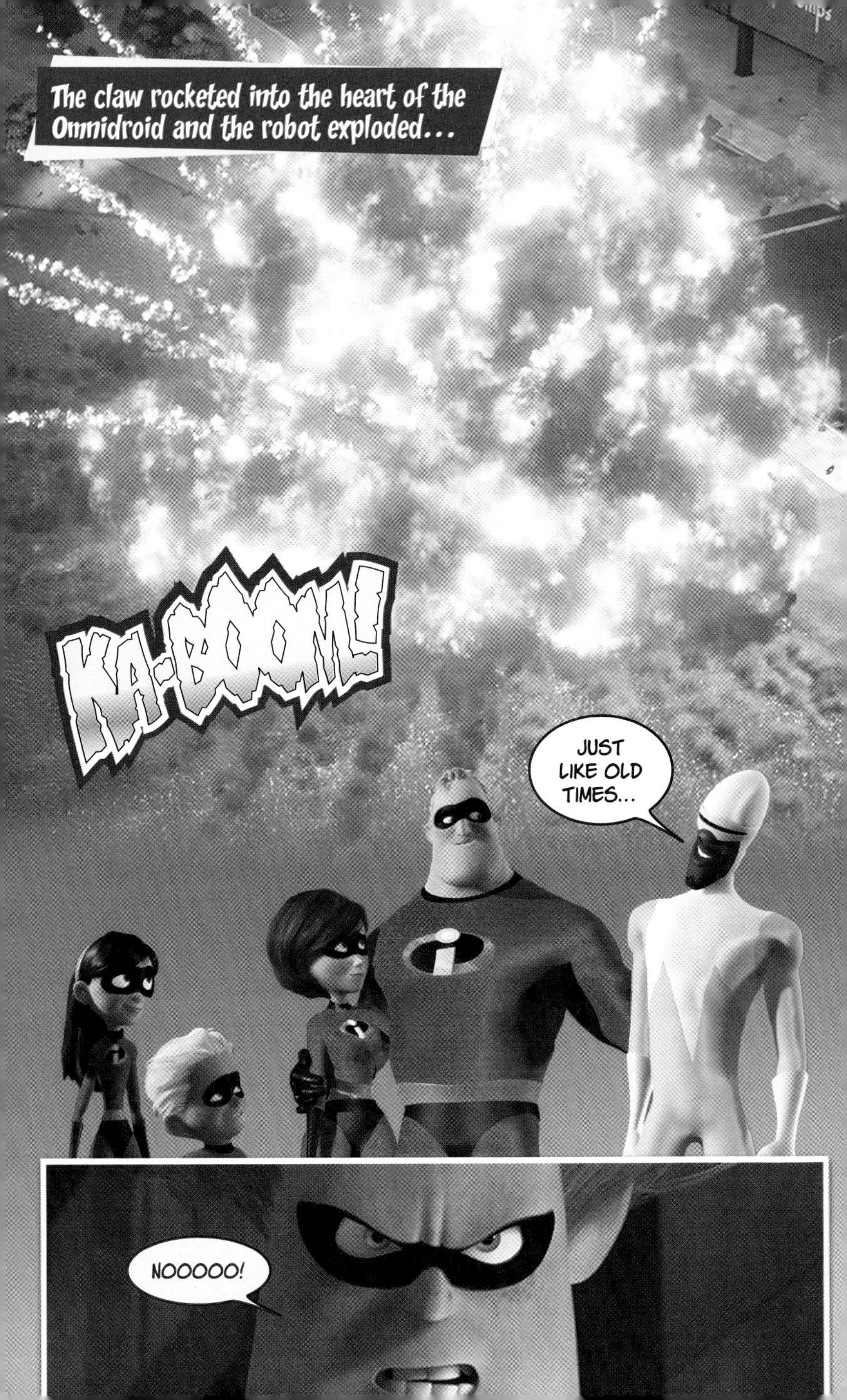
The claw rocketed into the heart of the Omnidroid and the robot exploded...
KA-BOOM!
JUST LIKE OLD TIMES...
NOOOOO!

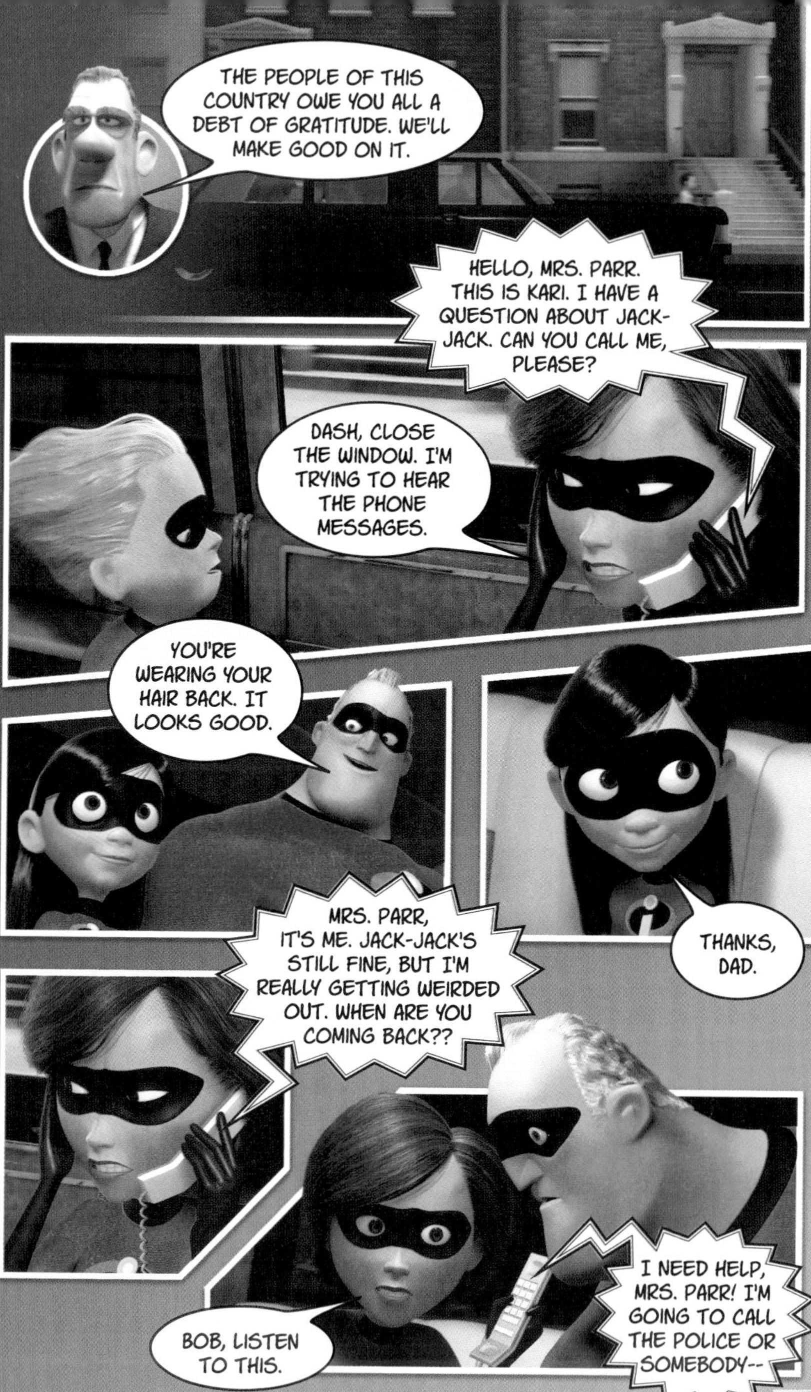
THE PEOPLE OF THIS COUNTRY OWE YOU ALL A DEBT OF GRATITUDE. WE'LL MAKE GOOD ON IT.
HELLO, MRS. PARR. THIS IS KARI. I HAVE A QUESTION ABOUT JACK-JACK. CAN YOU CALL ME, PLEASE?
DASH, CLOSE THE WINDOW. I'M TRYING TO HEAR THE PHONE MESSAGES.
YOU'RE WEARING YOUR HAIR BACK. IT LOOKS GOOD.
THANKS, DAD.
MRS. PARR, IT'S ME. JACK-JACK'S STILL FINE, BUT I'M REALLY GETTING WEIRDED OUT. WHEN ARE YOU COMING BACK??
BOB, LISTEN TO THIS.
I NEED HELP, MRS. PARR! I'M GOING TO CALL THE POLICE OR SOMEBODY--

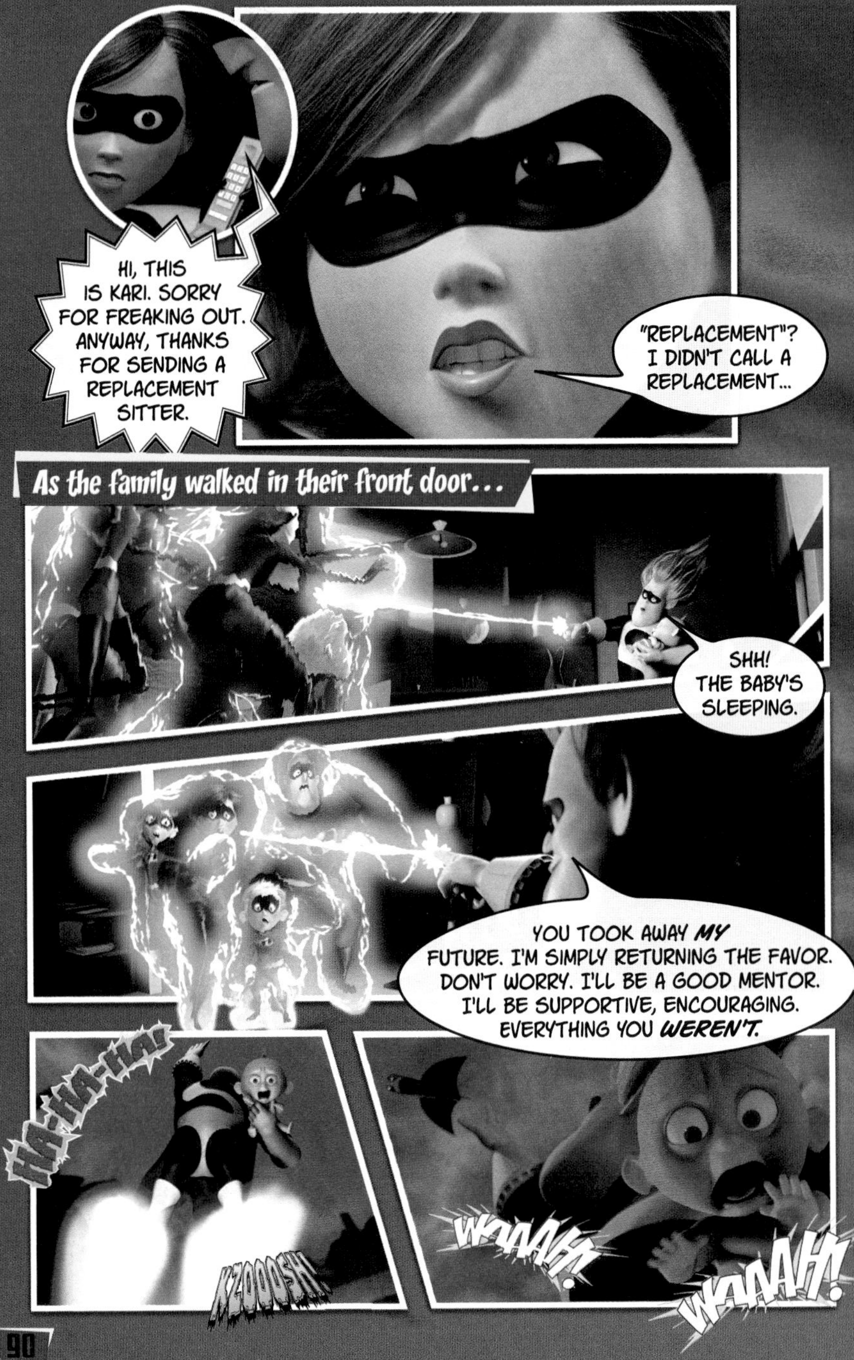
HI, THIS IS KARI. SORRY FOR FREAKING OUT. ANYWAY, THANKS FOR SENDING A REPLACEMENT SITTER.
"REPLACEMENT"? I DIDN'T CALL A REPLACEMENT...
As the family walked in their front door...
SHH! THE BABY'S SLEEPING.
YOU TOOK AWAY *MY* FUTURE. I'M SIMPLY RETURNING THE FAVOR. DON'T WORRY. I'LL BE A GOOD MENTOR. I'LL BE SUPPORTIVE, ENCOURAGING. EVERYTHING YOU ***WEREN'T.***
HA-HA-HA!
KZOOOSH!
WAAAH!
WAAAH!

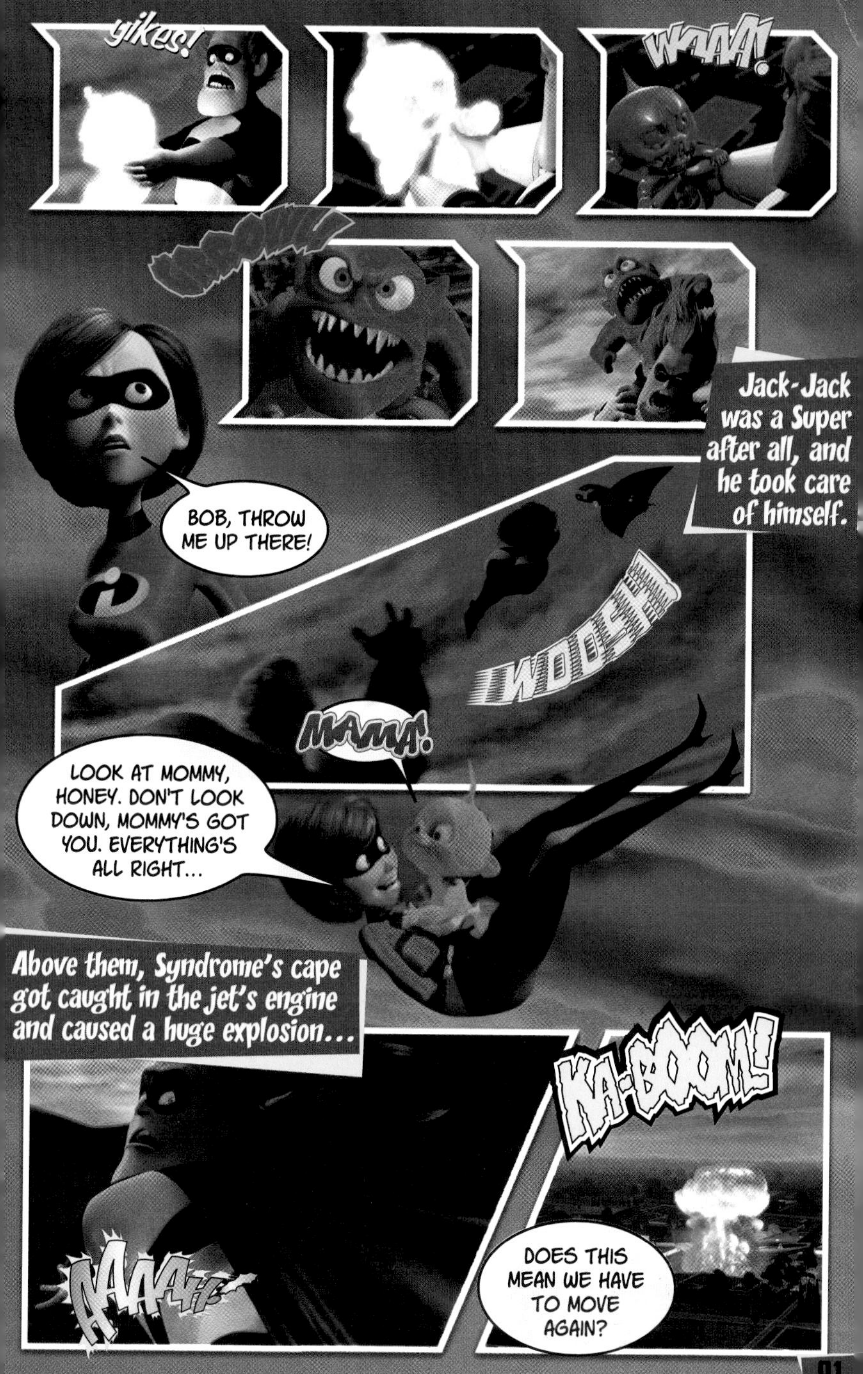

yikes!
WAAA!
Jack-Jack was a Super after all, and he took care of himself.
BOB, THROW ME UP THERE!
WOOSH!
MAMA!
LOOK AT MOMMY, HONEY. DON'T LOOK DOWN, MOMMY'S GOT YOU. EVERYTHING'S ALL RIGHT...
Above them, Syndrome's cape got caught in the jet's engine and caused a huge explosion...
KA-BOOM!
AAAAH!
DOES THIS MEAN WE HAVE TO MOVE AGAIN?

A few weeks later...

THE SPARTANS

ELEMENTARY SCHOOL
CITY TRACK FINALS

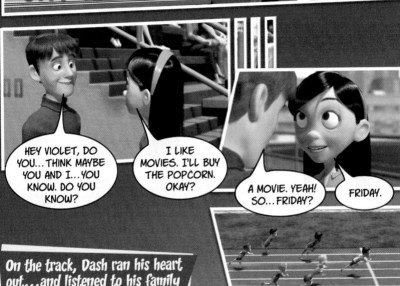

HEY VIOLET, DO YOU...THINK MAYBE YOU AND I...YOU KNOW. DO YOU KNOW?

I LIKE MOVIES. I'LL BUY THE POPCORN. OKAY?

A MOVIE. YEAH! SO...FRIDAY?

FRIDAY.

On the track, Dash ran his heart out...and listened to his family calling from the bleachers...

GO DASH, GO.

CLOSE SECOND!

MAKE IT CLOSE. SECOND PLACE!

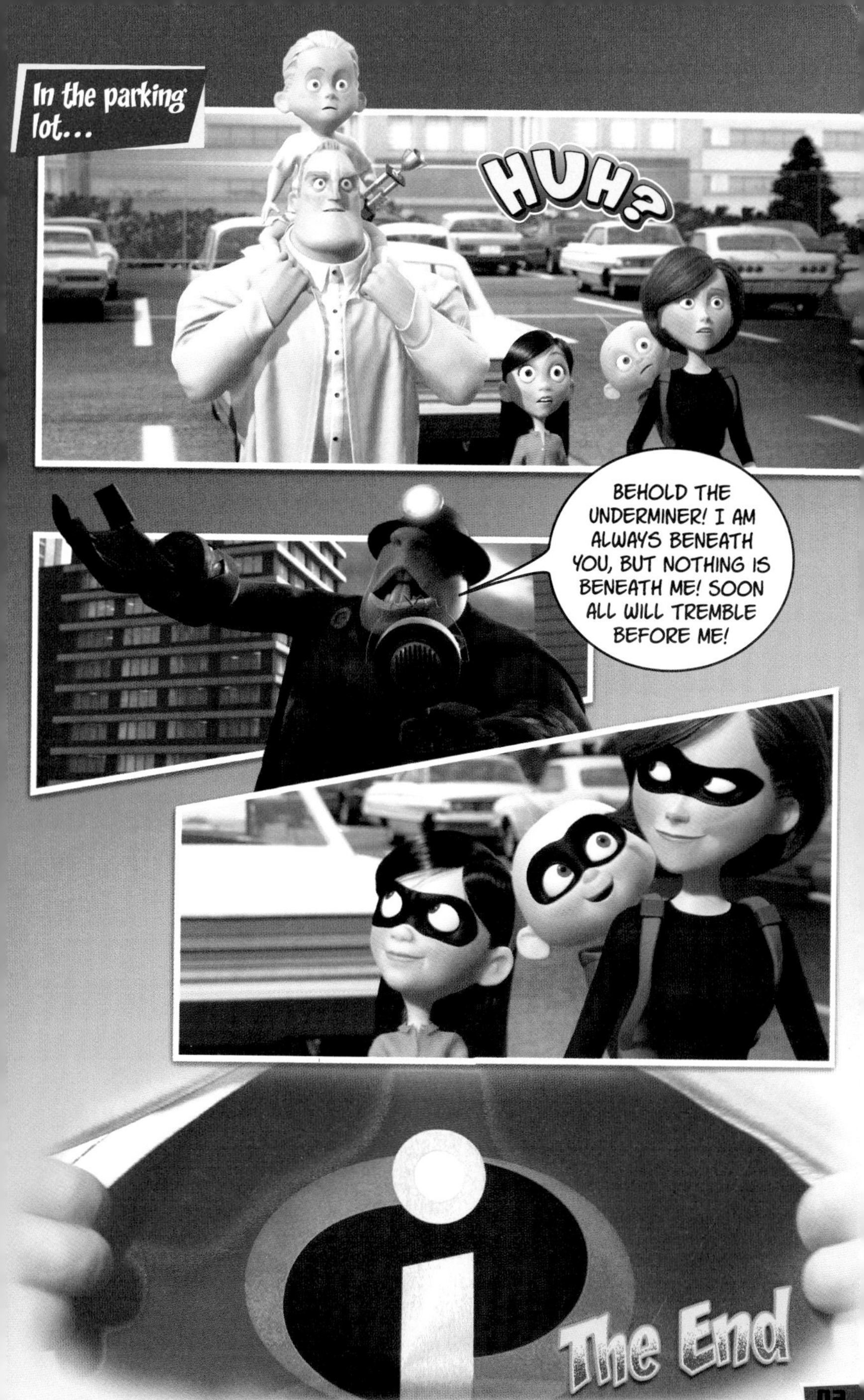
In the parking lot...
HUH?
BEHOLD THE UNDERMINER! I AM ALWAYS BENEATH YOU, BUT NOTHING IS BENEATH ME! SOON ALL WILL TREMBLE BEFORE ME!
The End

ALSO AVAILABLE FROM ☺TOKYOPOP®

MANGA

.HACK//LEGEND OF THE TWILIGHT
ALICHINO
ANGELIC LAYER
BABY BIRTH
BRAIN POWERED
BRIGADOON
B'TX
CANDIDATE FOR GODDESS, THE
CARDCAPTOR SAKURA
CARDCAPTOR SAKURA - MASTER OF THE CLOW
CHRONICLES OF THE CURSED SWORD
CLAMP SCHOOL DETECTIVES
CLOVER
COMIC PARTY
CORRECTOR YUI
COWBOY BEBOP
COWBOY BEBOP: SHOOTING STAR
CRESCENT MOON
CROSS
CULDCEPT
CYBORG 009
D•N•ANGEL
DEARS
DEMON DIARY
DEMON ORORON, THE
DIGIMON
DIGIMON TAMERS
DIGIMON ZERO TWO
DRAGON HUNTER
DRAGON KNIGHTS
DRAGON VOICE
DREAM SAGA
DUKLYON: CLAMP SCHOOL DEFENDERS
ET CETERA
ETERNITY
FAERIES' LANDING
FLCL
FLOWER OF THE DEEP SLEEP
FORBIDDEN DANCE
FRUITS BASKET
G GUNDAM
GATEKEEPERS
GIRL GOT GAME
GUNDAM SEED ASTRAY
GUNDAM SEED ASTRAY R
GUNDAM WING
GUNDAM WING: BATTLEFIELD OF PACIFISTS
GUNDAM WING: ENDLESS WALTZ
GUNDAM WING: THE LAST OUTPOST (G-UNIT)
HANDS OFF!

HARLEM BEAT
HYPER RUNE
I.N.V.U.
INITIAL D
INSTANT TEEN: JUST ADD NUTS
JING: KING OF BANDITS
JING: KING OF BANDITS - TWILIGHT TALES
JULINE
KARE KANO
KILL ME, KISS ME
KINDAICHI CASE FILES, THE
KING OF HELL
KODOCHA: SANA'S STAGE
LAGOON ENGINE
LEGEND OF CHUN HYANG, THE
LILING-PO
LOVE OR MONEY
MAGIC KNIGHT RAYEARTH I
MAGIC KNIGHT RAYEARTH II
MAN OF MANY FACES
MARMALADE BOY
MARS
MARS: HORSE WITH NO NAME
MINK
MIRACLE GIRLS
MODEL
MOURYOU KIDEN: LEGEND OF THE NYMPH
NECK AND NECK
ONE
ONE I LOVE, THE
PEACH FUZZ
PEACH GIRL
PEACH GIRL: CHANGE OF HEART
PHD: PHANTASY DEGREE
PITA-TEN
PLANET BLOOD
PLANET LADDER
PLANETES
PRESIDENT DAD
PRINCESS AI
PSYCHIC ACADEMY
QUEEN'S KNIGHT, THE
RAGNAROK
RAVE MASTER
REALITY CHECK
REBIRTH
REBOUND
RISING STARS OF MANGA™,THE
SAILOR MOON
SAINT TAIL
SAMURAI GIRL™ REAL BOUT HIGH SCHOOL

10.19.04

ALSO AVAILABLE FROM TOKYOPOP®

SOUL TO SEOUL
SEIKAI TRILOGY, THE
SGT. FROG
SHAOLIN SISTERS
SHIRAHIME-SYO: SNOW GODDESS TALES
SHUTTERBOX
SKULL MAN, THE
SUIKODEN III
SUKI
TAROT CAFÉ, THE
THREADS OF TIME
TOKYO BABYLON
TOKYO MEW MEW
VAMPIRE GAME
WARCRAFT
WISH
WORLD OF HARTZ
ZODIAC P.I.

CINE-MANGA®

ALADDIN
CARDCAPTORS
DUEL MASTERS
FAIRLY ODDPARENTS, THE
FAMILY GUY
FINDING NEMO
G.I. JOE SPY TROOPS
GREATEST STARS OF THE NBA
JACKIE CHAN ADVENTURES
JIMMY NEUTRON: BOY GENIUS, THE ADVENTURES OF
KIM POSSIBLE
LILO & STITCH: THE SERIES
LIZZIE MCGUIRE
LIZZIE MCGUIRE MOVIE, THE
MALCOLM IN THE MIDDLE
POWER RANGERS: DINO THUNDER
POWER RANGERS: NINJA STORM
PRINCESS DIARIES 2, THE
RAVE MASTER
SHREK 2
SIMPLE LIFE, THE
SPONGEBOB SQUAREPANTS
SPY KIDS 2
SPY KIDS 3-D: GAME OVER
TEENAGE MUTANT NINJA TURTLES
THAT'S SO RAVEN
TOTALLY SPIES
TRANSFORMERS: ARMADA
TRANSFORMERS: ENERGON

NOVELS

CLAMP SCHOOL PARANORMAL INVESTIGATORS
SAILOR MOON
SLAYERS

ART BOOKS

ART OF CARDCAPTOR SAKURA
ART OF MAGIC KNIGHT RAYEARTH, THE
PEACH: MIWA UEDA ILLUSTRATIONS

ANIME GUIDES

COWBOY BEBOP
GUNDAM TECHNICAL MANUALS
SAILOR MOON SCOUT GUIDES

TOKYOPOP KIDS

STRAY SHEEP

You want it? We got it!
A full range of TOKYOPOP products are available now at:
www.TOKYOPOP.com/shop

10.19.04Y

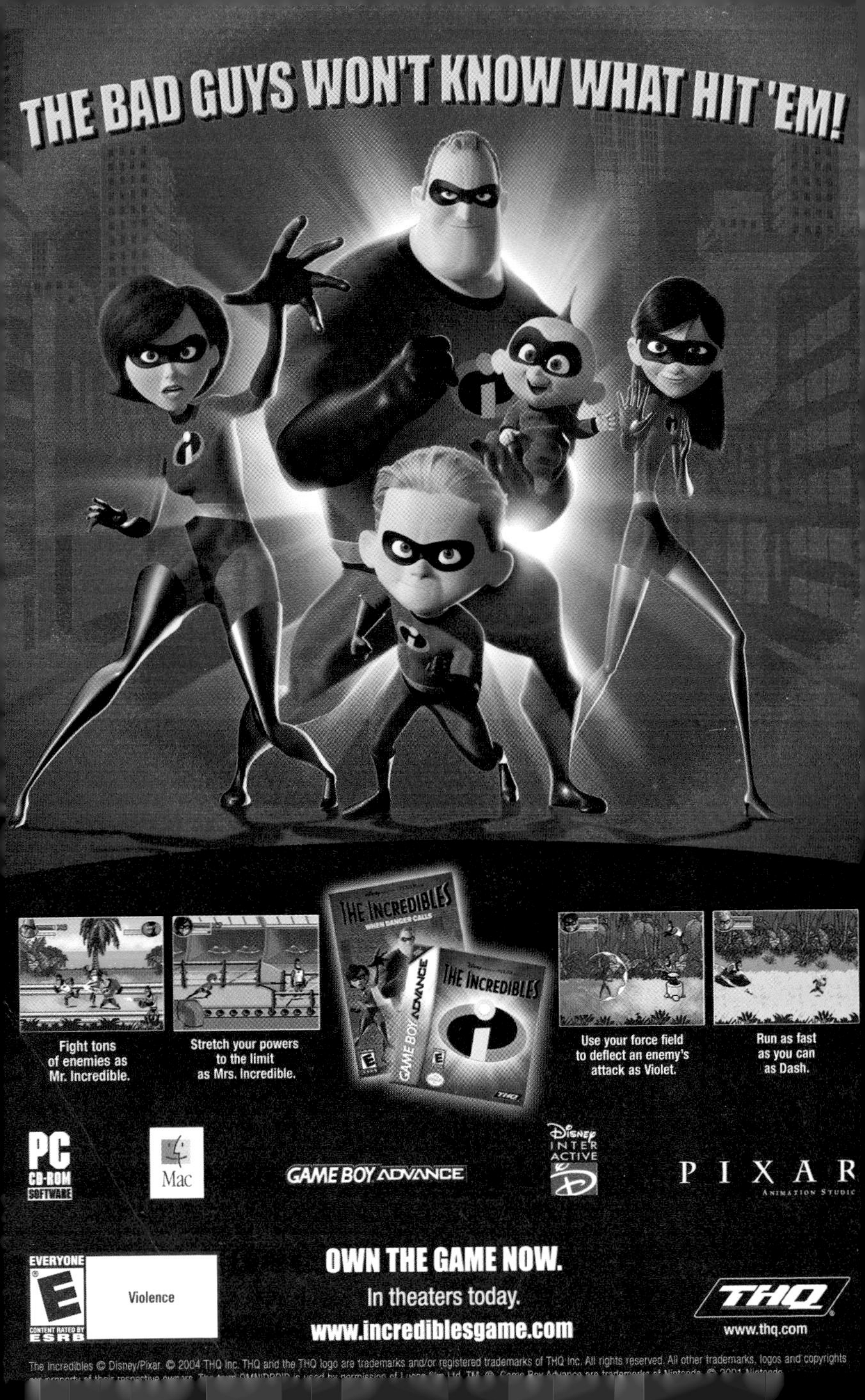
THE BAD GUYS WON'T KNOW WHAT HIT 'EM!
THE INCREDIBLES
WHEN DANGER CALLS
GAME BOY ADVANCE
THE INCREDIBLES
Fight tons of enemies as Mr. Incredible.
Stretch your powers to the limit as Mrs. Incredible.
Use your force field to deflect an enemy's attack as Violet.
Run as fast as you can as Dash.
PC CD-ROM SOFTWARE
Mac
GAME BOY ADVANCE
Disney INTERACTIVE
PIXAR ANIMATION STUDIOS
EVERYONE
E
CONTENT RATED BY ESRB
Violence
OWN THE GAME NOW.
In theaters today.
www.incrediblesgame.com
THQ
www.thq.com
The Incredibles © Disney/Pixar. © 2004 THQ Inc. THQ and the THQ logo are trademarks and/or registered trademarks of THQ Inc. All rights reserved. All other trademarks, logos and copyrights